SPIES, POLITICS, AND POWER

El Departamento Confidencial en México, 1922–1946

SPIES, POLITICS, AND POWER

El Departamento Confidencial en México, 1922–1946

Joseph A. Stout Jr.

TCU
PRESS

TCU Press

Fort Worth, Texas

Library of Congress Cataloging-in-Publication Data

Stout, Joseph Allen.
Spies, politics, and power : el Departamento Confidencial en México, 1922-1946 / Joseph A. Stout Jr.
   p. cm.
 Includes bibliographical references and index.
 ISBN 978-0-87565-438-6 (pbk. : alk. paper)
1. Mexico. Departamento Confidencial--History. 2. Intelligence service--Mexico--History--20th century. 3. Espionage--Mexico--History--20th century. 4. Internal security--Mexico--History--20th century. 5. Opposition (Political science)--Mexico--History--20th century. 6. Mexico--Politics and government--1910-1946. I. Title.
 JL1229.I6S76 2011
 327.1272009041--dc23
                     2011019636

TCU Press
P. O. Box 298300
Fort Worth, Texas 76129
817.257.7822
www.prs.tcu.edu

To order books: 1.800.826.8911

Designed by Vicki Whistler

CONTENTS

Preface   vii

Introduction   1

Chapter 1   Politics and Society to 1920   15

Chapter 2   El Departamento Confidencial, 1920–1930   31

Chapter 3   El Departamento Confidencial, 1930–1940   59

Chapter 4   National Security and the Departamento Confidencial, 1940–1946   105

Chapter 5   Conclusion   141

Notes   147

Bibliography   163

Index   169

About the Author   175

PREFACE

The focus of this study is the Departamento Confidencial (Confidential Department) of the Mexican government from 1922 to 1946. This secret agency, operating under the auspices of the Secretaría de Gobernación (Secretariat of Internal Political Affairs), sent operatives throughout the country to monitor social and political activities and identify potential threats to the central government.[1] Agent reports often contained an operative's interpretation of an individual's or group's loyalty to the regime and identified potential threats. While these reports provided valuable intelligence, occasionally incorrect information and speculation merged with fact and rendered some reports suspect. Initially inefficient, the agency never reached the level of effectiveness of internal monitoring agencies of many countries. Yet Gobernación increasingly professionalized the agency by instituting training programs and establishing guidelines for agents and reports.

My purpose in this study is to discuss the founding and organization of the Departamento Confidencial, explain its functions, assess its contribution to the maintenance of political and social stability, and evaluate its contribution to the concentration of political and military authority in Mexico City (Distrito Federal). Its role in institutionalizing the Mexican Revolution is implicit in the information provided.[2] Finally, I consider the agency's actions during World War II, when it focused its efforts on monitoring the activities of anyone of German, Japanese, or Italian ancestry, and played an important part in Mexico's relocation of those individuals of Axis heritage to areas where they could be more closely monitored.

While this agency's immediate purpose was the protection of the nation and a particular regime, it was also a useful central government weapon in the ongoing power struggle between regional caudillos and the national government. The conflict with local leaders furthermore involved the national government's efforts to change permanently some aspects of Mexican society. Many of these regional strongmen rose to power during the first fifty years of Mexico's independence from Spain (1821), a time when no consistent and efficient central authority existed. Local leaders used their wealth and position to protect their interests. These caudillos were colonial governors who had continued in their positions or assumed office after independence. They maintained local militia, often assumed the rank of general, and did whatever was needed to dominate a region. Factional conflict, decentralization, military coups, and civil war followed when reaching political consensus and establishing governmental legitimacy proved difficult.

In the 1870s, a regional caudillo, General Porfirio Díaz, assumed the presidency, where he remained for more than thirty years. His rule occurred, in part, as a consequence of threatening or coopting regional caudillos. However, most of these retained considerable power, continuing the tradition of local control. In 1910, with the onset of the Mexican Revolution, caudillismo reasserted itself with a vengeance, making centralizing authority in the Distrito Federal difficult.

The process of institutionalizing and centralizing power after the revolutionary violence of that period subsided has been a topic of importance for decades among those who have studied Mexico's institutional development and modernization. Political scientist Samuel P. Huntington suggested in his seminal work *Political Order in Changing Societies* that political systems could only be institutionalized after a government established authority over disparate elements in all sections of a country. Huntington spoke of political theory in modernizing states and devoted a chapter to Mexico.[3] Historians Mark Wasserman and Thomas Benjamin studied the problem of regional caudillo autonomy in their work *Provinces of the Revolution: Essays on Regional Mexican History, 1910–1929*, an edited collection containing articles by Wasserman, Benjamin, Romana Falcón, Paul Garner, Heather F. Salamini, Raymond Th. J. Buve, and Stuart Voss. Wasserman wrote in his contribution that to understand the Mexican Revolution—indeed, subsequent Mexican history—one has to look carefully at state and regional history. He suggested that despite their successes in centralizing control of the country during the 1920s and 1930s,

Presidents Alvaro Obregón and Plutarco Elías Calles were unable to "bring all of Mexico under their control."[4] Provincial leaders continued to create local, personal support by using patronage and threats, and by organizing the working class. As they had for generations, these caudillos threatened national sovereignty. Wasserman believed that while efforts to centralize control of Mexico had progressed by 1929, "the Mexican state was a long way from being all powerful."[5] He suggested that "the national, centralized state did not emerge until late in the Lázaro Cárdenas era, which lasted from 1934 to 1940."[6] The Departamento Confidencial, through internal monitoring of social and political activities, contributed to this ultimate centralizing of power in the Distrito Federal.

The majority of the documents I used for this study are in approximately three thousand archival boxes located in the Archivo General de la Nación (AGN), now housed in Lecumberri, the former prison of the Federal District. These documents were opened to investigators during 1998, the year I began research on this subject. Several scholars in Mexico assisted me during the six years I researched this study in the Distrito Federal. María de los Angeles Magdaleno Cárdenas has helped me more than anyone else south of the border. Angeles found and copied documents for me and shared her vast knowledge and considerable research. Lic. Norma Mireles de Ogarrio, Director of the Fideicomiso Archivos Plutarco Elías Calles y Fernando Torreblanca, provided information about presidents Elías Calles and Obregón. I also wish to thank Dra. Patricia Galeana Valadés, former Director of the AGN, who made it possible for me to examine documents related to the Departamento Confidencial. Lic. Jorge Nacif Mina, who was in charge of the materials I used at the AGN, assisted my efforts. Roberto Beristaín, who is now retired but knows more about the AGN than anyone else, helped me find documents that seemed forever lost. Lic. Roberto Marín Maldonado, former chief of the historical archive of the Secretariat of Foreign Relations (Archivo Histórico "Genaro Estrada" de la Secretaría de Relaciones Exteriores), supplied materials. For continued help in the writing of this manuscript, I owe a debt of gratitude to Dr. Michael M. Smith, who served for three decades as a mentor in my study of Mexican history, and to Dr. Douglas W. Richmond, who offered critical comments that greatly improved various parts of the manuscript.

Finally, I wish to thank Bonnie J. Stout for her support of my research and her patience while I spent many months each year in México, DF, or monopolized the computer at home. MacGregor, the family Westie, remained on the couch in my office and often let me know how bored he was with all of this.

Joseph A. Stout Jr.
Regents Professor Emeritus
Oklahoma State University, Stillwater

INTRODUCTION

For decades after gaining its independence from Spain in 1821, Mexico suffered intermittent political disorder until General Porfirio Díaz seized control of the country in the mid-1870s. He remained in power for more than three decades, bringing political stability and economic progress until May 1911, when Francisco I. Madero and other armed revolutionaries overthrew the old dictator. Later that year Madero won election to the presidency, a position he occupied until February 1913, when General Victoriano Huerta toppled his government and had Madero executed. Violence erupted anew throughout the country and continued unabated until 1915, when Governor Venustiano Carranza of Coahuila established himself as de facto president. Although opposing factions continued to oppose his efforts, Carranza oversaw the writing of a new constitution and assumed the presidency in 1917. Unfortunately, the struggle for power did not end. Many regional caudillos refused to accept either Carranza's election or his policies, and violence persisted. In 1920, Carranza's rivals assassinated him after he attempted to manipulate the election of Ignacio Bonillas, his handpicked civilian successor, to the presidency.

Successive Mexican governments sought to reorder society, institutionalize reforms, and extend central government control to rural Mexico. To accomplish these changes, presidents Alvaro Obregón, Plutarco Elías Calles, and Lázaro Cárdenas collectivized agriculture in many areas; attacked the Catholic Church, including its domination of education; nationalized several industries; interfered with local village activities; and created a national political party with the aim of forcing all areas outside Mexico City to defer to the national government in contests of power and policy. The national government occasionally harassed businesses and closed newspapers whose editors opposed the government. Frequently, large landowners (hacendados), local politicians, religious leaders, and military officers opposed changes that threatened their role in society and took up arms to battle the central government. Between 1920 and 1946, opposition to national efforts to restructure society persisted. Post-1920 central government leaders responded to this opposition, armed and otherwise, by sending loyal army troops to battle the dissenters. They also created new agencies to monitor political, social, and military opposition throughout the country.

During the extended military phase of the Mexican Revolution (1911–1920), the collection of information concerning the activities of opposing armed factions and political dissidents had played a significant role in determining who would win the struggle for control of the country. Military and civilian leaders wanted to know what their enemies were doing at all times. To gather various types of intelligence, they sent military and civilian agents into opposition-dominated territories, a strategy that became an accepted practice of Mexico's central government. After President Alvaro Obregón (1920–1924) appointed General Plutarco Elías Calles as Secretario de Gobernación, Calles began the systematic organization of the Departamento Confidencial as a professional domestic intelligence-gathering agency that would survive far beyond the immediate postrevolutionary period. Calles served as president from 1924 to 1928 and expanded the use of internal surveillance; he sent a signal to Mexicans brazen enough to oppose him or the government that they could suffer consequences for any behavior he considered subversive. Although Calles did not personally eliminate opponents, some indiscreet enough to oppose him died mysteriously, while others merely lost their government jobs or were sufficiently intimidated to cease opposition. Subsequent chief executives continued to employ the Departamento Confidencial as one of the forces to consolidate and maintain their authority. The department was more important than such an agency might have been in countries with a well-organized national police force. Mexican leaders relied on political, social, and military intelligence to protect their regimes, and, ultimately, they turned to military force to suppress opposition.

Ascension to or retention of political power, or changing social or political behavior in any nation, depends upon popular support, a powerful military, the level of violence a government is willing to use, and gathering information about the activities of real or potential enemies. Historically, governments have routinely employed domestic surveillance and foreign espionage to maintain power. Military leaders have dispatched spies into enemy territory to gather intelligence about troop strength, deployment, and morale. Civilian leaders have employed agents within the country to uncover antigovernment plots, stifle free speech, and, when necessary, intimidate the population through violence. Agents also have gathered information aimed at ruining a political opponent's reputation or to employ blackmail. Finally, internal surveillance has proven deadly to enemies of governments whose agents monitor political and social behavior and mark certain individuals for elimination or incarceration. In order to place political surveillance in Mexico between 1920 and 1946 within a broader comparative context, it is instructive to outline the gathering and utilization of internal intelligence at approximately the same time in Russia (in both the pre-Stalinist and Soviet periods), Nazi Germany, and the United States.

After overthrowing the Russian czar in December 1917, Bolshevik revolutionaries realized that to remain in power, to curtail any thoughts of democracy, and to make basic changes in society, they needed to develop intelligence-gathering agencies to monitor all activities within the country. Although the Communists continued military intelligence gathering that the czarist government had established, they created new internal monitoring agencies and changed existing ones to bring about the societal changes the Communists desired. This reordering of society included an attack on religion to weaken its influence on individuals and the substitution of an atheistic state. The government demanded that religions register their organizations with the state; it closed churches, murdered clergy, and destroyed church buildings. The Communists sought nothing less than the eradication of religions. Josef Stalin, the brutal dictator of the Soviet Union for decades, ordered the killing of approximately twenty million Russian Orthodox Church members and several million more of other religions. Other changes in Soviet society included the collectivization of agriculture to achieve political control of rural regions and increase production, the seizure of private property, the suppression of private enterprise, and the insistence that the state maintain the power to build a better national infrastructure.

As a part of a totalitarian regime determined to reorder society, internal espionage agencies were vitally important in the Soviet Union. Their use and refinement led to more pervasive persecution of ordinary citizens. The Bolsheviks not only spied on residents of all regions of the country, they also initiated a reign of terror against military personnel and civilians alike, intimidating, murdering, and imprisoning anyone they suspected of posing a threat. To carry out its programs, the government established the CHEKA (All-Russian Extraordinary Commission for Combating Counter-Revolution and Sabotage), a secret political department with police powers designed to spy upon the general population. The CHEKA's brutal methods provoked widespread popular opposition to the regime. Dissidents protested the agency's actions by organizing strikes and other antigovernment demonstrations. The CHEKA retaliated, murdering hundreds of innocent people and "disappearing" more into prisons or slave-labor work camps without trials or bringing formal charges against them. The Soviet people responded so negatively to such tactics that the Bolsheviks superficially modified their methods. The revisions, however, were purely cosmetic.

In 1923, Stalin officially established the USSR (Union of Soviet Socialist Republics) and consolidated his control of the new federation of Soviet states. No area of the country escaped his oversight. After 1929, he initiated a broadened pogrom against all dissidents; as a consequence, his agents murdered perhaps twenty million peasants and regular army officers and exiled more to work camps in Siberia. The persecution of Soviet citizens became more pervasive each year. Agents spied on civilians, ordinary citizens spied on each other, and the spies passed on their information to various government agencies. In 1932, Stalin integrated a reorganized OGPU (the State Political Directorate, which was the secret police) into the GUGB (Chief Directorate for State Security) and once again placed it under the NKVD (the People's Commissariat for Internal Affairs, a key agency of political repression). This powerful organization controlled conventional police forces, border guards, internal troops, and concentration and labor camps, as well as much of the transportation system and many businesses.

By 1938, when Stalin named L. P. Beria, who had spent twenty-one years directing provincial purges, to head of the NKVD, no civil liberties remained in the Soviet Union. Government agents opened private letters, tapped phone lines, and used informants to monitor citizen behavior. By

1941, NKVD controlled most Soviet industries, many of which utilized forced labor programs the agency designed and directed. That year the Soviets again separated the GUGB from the NKVD. The now-independent political police organization was renamed the NKGB (People's Commissariat for State Security). Five years later, the NKVD and NKGB were elevated to the status of government ministries. During the 1940s, the NKGB became the KGB (Committee for State Security). Although the KGB and its predecessors included some well-trained agents, at first most were rank amateurs. A few diplomats, foreign trade representatives, news agency correspondents, and others served the organization under its various titles and incarnations. Although the KGB agents operated in foreign countries, Stalin most frequently employed the agency as a police force to suppress or control the Soviet people.

Between 1933 and 1945, the German government under Adolf Hitler and the National Socialist Party (Nazi) also sought to reorganize almost every aspect of society. Changes brought Nazification of education that included emphasis on physical training, sports, state and Hitler worship, and biology. The Nazi instructors twisted biology to fit their racial and nationalistic perspectives; Nazi ideology was anti-intellectual, subordinated females, and deliberately attempted to break down family structure with the Hitler Youth movement. The Nazis also confiscated some agricultural lands and put these into the hands of small farmers in order to encourage the rural poor to support the state. Nazi leadership believed these farmers were the backbone of agricultural production and the ultimate source of racial purity. Other Nazi changes inaugurated strict government control of business with the goal of ramping up industrial production and dictating monetary policy. Nazi agents in all realms of business monitored industrial output, outlawed labor unions, scrutinized banking activities, and tolerated no deviation from Hitler's policies. Finally, the Nazis ended freedom of the press and attacked organized religions, killing hundreds of thousands of religious people who refused to cease public worship.

Nazi programs aroused opposition from almost every sector of Germany. Dozens of small groups continued pressure through civic defiance wherever possible. Many German males eighteen years and younger refused to join the Hitler Youth and created cells of resistance. The government drafted all eighteen-year-old men into the army, but many continued their opposition to the Nazis. Retired army officers and a large sector of the German aristocracy, many of whom were members of both groups, plotted to overthrow Hitler.

When facing resistance to his programs, Hitler used any available means to spy on and intimidate the population. He reorganized existing government internal security agencies and created new political police or internal spy agencies to control the country. These organizations monitored all political and social activities, infiltrated anti-Nazi groups, and became instrumental in eliminating opposition. The Nazis continually strengthened the Secret State Police (Gestapo), an agency that greatly resembled the Soviet KGB, but operated more efficiently. More importantly, the Gestapo functioned with the general compliance of the German people, which contributed to its effectiveness. Even before Hitler came to power, several German state governments had created secret police organizations. Soon after he became chancellor of Germany in 1933, Hitler established himself as the unquestionable leader (Der Fuhrer) of the nation. To carry out his nefarious plan to reorder German society and to protect his position, he turned to Heinrich Himmler, a sadistic Nazi insider who had ingratiated himself with Hitler during his tenure as chief of the party SS (Schutzstaffel or "Protective Squadron"), a security organization that spied on fellow Nazis and enforced party directives through violence. Ultimately, the SS became Himmler's personal army.

In 1933, Himmler created the ORPO (Uniformed or Order Police) and the SIPO (Security Police), a plainclothes detective agency that operated independently. Himmler systematically seized control of the various state Gestapo organizations and centralized their administration. The following year, and with Hitler's blessings, Himmler incorporated all state police entities into the Gestapo. The organization was now a full-fledged national police force. The goal of this reorganization was to detect any threat to the Nazi regime. Cooperating with Himmler in this endeavor was Reinhard Heydrich, who tailored the Gestapo into a brutal secret state police agency. At first, the organization was staffed largely with professionally trained operatives. As time passed, however, Himmler and his Nazi party hacks filled the ranks, bringing a drastic decline in the quality of agents, their morality, and their work.

Gestapo agents knew that their primary function was to spy on fellow Germans. In addition to assigning them the task of handling routine legal and administrative affairs, Himmler ordered them to infiltrate suspicious or unsanctioned social gatherings. He also assigned one highly secret division of the Gestapo to ferret out disloyalty by spying on Marxists, "reactionaries," foreigners, and Jews. The agency built extensive, detailed files on these and other groups and organizations considered to be security risks. By 1937, Himmler and Heydrich had thoroughly "Nazified" all German security organizations. The next year Himmler determined that suitable policemen should become SS members, thereby tying them directly to the Nazi party.

Himmler and Heydrich carefully organized Gestapo spying operations down to the city-block level. Many Germans willingly collaborated with the Gestapo, reporting any statements or conversations deemed derogatory to Hitler or the Nazi Party. Gestapo agents systematically compiled an extensive and detailed file of rumors and catalogued any questionable activity. By the late 1930s, Himmler had extended Gestapo operations into the international arena, sending cadres of German spies into numerous countries in Europe, Africa, North America, and Latin America, including Mexico. (Such activities provoked an ongoing conflict with Admiral Wilhelm Canaris, head of the prestigious Abwehr [German Military Intelligence]). Before the outbreak of World War II, the Departamento Confidencial and other Mexican agencies already had begun to identify and monitor German activities in Mexico.

While the foregoing overview of the Soviet and German internal security agencies outlines how such organizations functioned in totalitarian regimes, a few comments about the United States Federal Bureau of Investigation (FBI) during the period under consideration provides insight into the operations of a domestic law enforcement and intelligence-gathering agency in a democratic state relatively similar to Mexico. Domestic surveillance in the United States originated with military intelligence operations in the early years of the republic. Later, the Department of the Treasury employed special agents to investigate currency crimes and other violations of federal law. During the Civil War, both sides sent agents into enemy territory to determine troop dispositions and appraise public morale. In 1865, the Department of the Treasury formally established a "Secret Service Department" to suppress the rampant counterfeiting of federal currency. In the postwar years, the army occupied the former rebellious states to ensure they accepted the military verdict. The army and civilian bureaucrats enforced congressional Reconstruction programs and insured local compliance with federal laws and regulations. During Reconstruction, military and civilian agents as well as paid informers maintained surveillance of southern politicians and ordinary citizens. In 1870, Congress created the Department of Justice to investigate federal crimes of all types. As it initially had no agents of its own, the agency borrowed operatives from the Department of the Treasury to conduct investigations. Until the twentieth century, therefore, internal espionage in the United States was primarily left to agents of the Departments of War and Treasury.

On July 26, 1908, responsibility for such clandestine operations changed significantly when Attorney General Charles J. Bonaparte created the Bureau of Investigation, a precursor of the modern Federal Bureau of Investigation. The new unit, operating under the Department of Justice, hired thirty-four employees who comprised what Bonaparte called the "Special Agent Force." President Theodore Roosevelt had encouraged the creation of the agency to investigate certain types of federal crimes and widespread corruption in Congress. Meanwhile, agents of the Department of the Treasury continued to assist in investigations of financial fraud, violations of United States neutrality laws, and other crimes deemed federal in nature. Roosevelt also ordered Treasury agents to investigate the unlawful exploitation of the nation's natural resources and the monopolistic practices of capitalist enterprises. By 1910, the Bureau of Investigation had taken on additional responsibilities, expanded to a force of sixty-four agents, and exercised a growing level of power and authority. To some extent, it was emerging as a national police organization. As a consequence, some critics feared that the agency was becoming a secret state police force incompatible with a democratic form of government.

In 1914, war broke out between France and Germany and quickly spread to Britain and the rest of continental Europe. By 1917, it had become a global conflict. Until that year, the United States officially remained neutral; however, public sentiment generally favored England and its allies over Germany and the rest of the Central Powers. By 1915, German and Austrian agents in the United States were engaging in espionage, financing anti-British propaganda campaigns, organizing strikes in various war-related industries, and committing acts of sabotage. In response, United States agents tracked German clandestine operatives, conducted counterespionage operations, and profiled enemy aliens and suspected US citizens alike. Reacting to the growing paranoia roused by incidents of German sabotage and perceived threats to national security by domestic political radicals, Congress enacted the Alien Act (1917) and the Sedition Act (1918). The new legislation gave federal authorities extensive power to combat internal enemies by limiting or abrogating their freedom of speech and association, especially those individuals or groups who opposed United States involvement in the war.

The postwar years brought new developments on the US intelligence-gathering front. During this period, the activities of Communists and other radical groups fostered a "Red Scare," heightening concerns about national security. The Bolshevik revolution and the subsequent development of a Communist government in Russia elevated the rising fear of subversion in the United States to new heights. As a consequence, in 1919, United States Attorney General A. Mitchell Palmer created a special division within the Department of Justice to investigate such threats, catalogue information about radical groups and organizations, and mark "dangerous" individuals for deportation. J. Edgar Hoover, an enterprising twenty-four-year-old Department of Justice lawyer, compiled a list of four hundred thousand people deemed dangerous to the country. The suspects included innocent American citizens, prominent politicians who had opposed the war, and numerous others. Much of Hoover's data was based on mere hearsay or rumor; nevertheless, he treated the information as fact and acted accordingly. At the same time, Hoover added a parallel file for his personal use that he maintained until his death in 1972.

In 1935, Congress officially changed the name of the agency to the Federal Bureau of Investigation (FBI) and named Hoover its first director. In addition to its crime-fighting tasks, President Franklin D. Roosevelt ordered the FBI to identify and closely monitor the movements of Nazi agents and to investigate Communist activities in the United States. In 1940, to strengthen the FBI in its efforts, the president and Congress allowed the bureau to tap private phone lines, intercept personal postal and telegraphic communications, and ignore other constitutional protections of United States citizens.

Hoover assumed the authority to collect and file personal information about any person in the country, further violating privacy guarantees. Such information regarding public officials' illicit sexual liaisons, drunk driving or illegal drug use, and other instances of moral transgression could and would be used against anyone who questioned his authority or opposed him. In December 1941, after the United States entered World War II, the FBI added the task of foreign intelligence gathering to its domestic responsibilities, and agents were assigned to numerous international stations, including several in Mexico. In the United States, Hoover instructed his agents to intercept and open the mail of opponents of Roosevelt's policies and American involvement in World War II, including well-known Senator Gerald K. Nye of North Dakota.

During the war, the FBI also played an important role in the forcible relocation to detention camps of tens of thousands of persons of Japanese descent, whose loyalty to the United States became highly suspect after Japan bombed the United States naval base at Pearl Harbor, Hawaii. It meant little that most of the detainees were United States citizens. Men, women, and children were forced to remain in these camps until almost the end of the war. Treated as enemy aliens, detained Japanese and Japanese Americans were not allowed to leave the camps, except for the hundreds who (ironically) joined the United States armed forces and fought in the European theater. While in confinement, resident Japanese and Japanese American families experienced financial ruin and the loss of their civil rights and human dignity.

After Allied victory in the war, a new chapter in FBI operations began. President Harry S. Truman ordered the FBI to cease its operations in foreign countries and restricted its authority in domestic concerns. The president's authority was based on congressional creation of the Central Intelligence Agency, provided for in the National Security Act of 1947. By this time, the major concern of the United States was the spread of international communism as the former Soviet Union moved to control all of Eastern Europe and much of Asia.

It is evident from this brief overview of monitoring national security in the United States that the FBI focused on internal security in times of war and at other times fought criminal activities. The agency did not usually become involved in perpetuating a regime, although FDR had used it to monitor some of his political opponents. Furthermore, there is no evidence that an FBI investigation led directly to the death of an opponent of the ruling political party, although political assassinations surely occurred.

The Gestapo, KGB, FBI, and Departamento Confidencial contributed to concentrating and strengthening the power of their respective governments. Consequently, each agency contributed to institutional development, modernization, and change in their respective societies. The methods they used to collect information and the efficiency of the agencies varied; the ultimate use of that information ranged from benign to fatal. During World War II, the Departamento Confidencial and the FBI operated in similar fashion regarding their treatment of people of Japanese descent. Both agencies monitored the activities of all people with Axis ties, and both played a significant role in relocating the Japanese to areas where they could be monitored. In the United States, only the Japanese were confined forcibly to relocation camps, far from coastal areas. They lost homes and businesses, careers, and freedom of movement. In Mexico, the Departamento Confidencial was likewise involved in relocating the Japanese away from the coasts, and many were forced to leave possessions and property just as in the United States. In Mexico, however, the Japanese were not held in camps. Nonetheless, they could not travel about or leave Mexico City or wherever they had been confined. Mexico did attempt to confine the movements of Germans and Italians as well, but not as severely as those of the Japanese.

In contrast to the containment strategies used by US and Mexican intelligence agencies, the Soviet and German governments employed the KGB and Gestapo to assist in eliminating populations determined to be a threat to central government power or for purposes of "ethnic cleansing," the Nazi euphemism for the annihilation of Jews, gypsies, and others deemed inferior. The Mexican and US governments did not use the Departamento Confidencial or the FBI for such sinister aims; however, the Mexican agency adopted a stance toward religious institutions that mirrored the Soviet's. While the Nazis largely accommodated the Catholic, Lutheran, and other major religious groups, the Soviets pitted the KGB against churches and sent KGB agents undercover as newspaper reporters and under other false identities to spy on almost everything in the country. Likewise, in Mexico, Plutarco Elías Calles sought to end the influence of the Catholic Church, especially in the political sector, thus provoking church opposition in the form of the Cristero Rebellion of 1926 to 1929. The Mexican government responded, sending agents of the Departamento Confidencial to monitor actions of the Catholic clergy and supporters of the Catholic Church. This confrontation led to many deaths.

Between 1917 and 1946, Mexico, Nazi Germany, the Soviet Union, and the United States sporadically experienced change. From 1910 to 1917, Mexico and the Soviet Union suffered political and social revolutions that destabilized political institutions and reorganized society. Governments in each country during the next decades were determined to bring political stability and reorder society to correspond with new political and social views. The world economic depression that began with the United States stock market crash of 1929 also provoked changes in all of these countries. Political power brokers capitalized on the ensuing social and political unrest to change the way their governments sought the support of their citizens. These changes led to opposition from groups across the political spectrum.

In order to win the battle for change and remain in power, governments turned to monitoring social, political, and military activities. As Mexico did not have a national police force such as the KGB or the Gestapo, or an organization patterned after the FBI, the Departamento Confidencial, a weaker and less efficient agency, was the major internal agency monitoring social and political conditions. The fact that this agency enjoyed no police powers, operated in a more open society, and never had the sinister reputation of the KGB or Gestapo made it much less threatening to the average citizen. No available documents show that the agency marked specific Mexicans to be eliminated. In addition, Mexican leaders tended to use force as a last resort, preferring negotiation to accomplish political and social compliance. Consequently, the government seemed less dictatorial or threatening, rarely provoking sustained resistance. In fact, Calles's attack on religion led to the most widespread public armed resistance, given that the majority of Mexicans were devout defenders of the Catholic Church, whether they attended regularly or not. Landowners and army officers who lost positions or property on occasion rebelled, but they did not have sufficient popular support to pose a long-term threat to the national government. Violence occurred, but not as frequently or pervasively as in Germany or the Soviet Union during the same period. While it did not have the powers or sinister reputation of the KGB or the Gestapo, however, the Departamento Confidencial helped to stabilize politics and institutionalize authority by identifying threats to the government.[1]

CHAPTER 1

POLITICS AND SOCIETY TO 1920

On September 16, 1810, at Dolores, Guanajuato, Padre Miguel Hidalgo y Costilla proclaimed his grito (call or cry) for liberty and equality under the law, thus giving formal expression to a movement that culminated in Mexico's independence from Spain. During the next eleven years, approximately six hundred thousand people perished before Mexico gained its independence. Who was going to govern Mexico, and by what means, proved difficult questions for insurrectionary factions and their heirs.

When Spanish authority collapsed in Mexico, Agustín de Iturbide temporarily enjoyed significant support. In February 1823, facing widespread rebellions, he resigned his self-appointed position of emperor. Upon his departure from office, little central or legitimate power existed to protect people and property or to govern the country. Filling this power vacuum were caudillos or strongmen, who briefly occupied the presidency or established control in their states. While these leaders provided intermittent stability, their influence made it ever more difficult for national leaders in Mexico City to govern the country. For much of the nineteenth century, the contest for power focused on factions that supported local rule in a federal system and those who wanted to centralize power in Mexico City. Regional caudillos frequently sought to extend their influence throughout the country. However, so little consistency and agreement existed among these chieftains that between 1833 and 1855 the Mexican presidency changed hands thirty-six times.[1]

General Porfirio Díaz, who occupied the presidency from 1876 to 1911, recognized the inherent regional desire to be independent of national government dictates. In order to modernize the country, he sought to centralize authority in Mexico City by coopting through various methods the army, the emerging middle class, and local leaders across the country. He rewarded regional strongmen who cooperated with his regime and transferred uncooperative governors and military commanders away from their power bases and eliminated or undermined those who proved recalcitrant.[2] He also forged an agreement with the Catholic Church whereby it would not meddle in politics. Díaz reciprocated by not enforcing anticlerical laws that threatened the church. Personally religious, he did not wish to harm the church; he was primarily interested in retaining power. During his reign, Mexico had phenomenal economic development as mineral production quadrupled, textile mills were built, railroads expanded, and oil production became a major source of revenue. Unfortunately, the gap between the rich and poor widened, and power and money were concentrated in the hands of a few. At the turn of the century, despite his efforts and the considerable economic development and modernization he brought to the country, Díaz faced increasing political opposition.

By 1900, opposition to Díaz was gaining strength and focus. Included in this movement were Ricardo Flores Magón and his brother Enrique, who were calling weekly in the periodical *Regeneración* for the removal of Díaz. The brothers posed an increasingly difficult problem for Díaz as they also founded the Partido Liberal Mexicano and generally fostered unrest, first in Mexico and later along the United States–Mexico border. In 1904, having been arrested several times and released in Mexico, the Flores Magón brothers fled to the United States, where they continued to call for the ouster of Díaz. They expanded their movement both geographically and ideologically into the lower Río Grande valley of Texas, calling for an end to "economic exploitation and ethnic discrimination against Mexicans and Mexican Americans in the Southwestern United States."[3] The United States government eventually imprisoned the brothers for violating United States neutrality laws. In 1922, Ricardo Flores Magón died in prison.

In addition to political problems, Díaz also faced widespread banditry in the country, particularly in the early phase of his regime. To counter this, he reorganized the *guardias rurales,* or federal police force, and enlarged it considerably. The organization was only partially successful, however, and while it suppressed some of the banditry, its methods were frequently brutal.[4]

Important to Díaz's survival during his long reign were the efforts of a secret service that he operated as an appendage of the Mexican consular system. Díaz used consular agents in the United States, especially along the binational border, to supply information about the activities of dissidents who had fled north of the border. These agents hired contract operatives to work along both sides of the border, and they also paid informants and well-known United States detective agencies to assist them in their efforts. Enrique Creel, who married into the wealthy Terrazas family in Chihuahua, and who had held numerous posts in the state and national government, was informally in charge of intelligence for the Díaz government. Creel hired the Furlong Secret Service Company, based in St. Louis, Missouri, to monitor political dissidents. Its principle, Thomas Furlong, generally sent agents to work along the United States side of the border, but he also dispatched them into Mexico to gather information.[5]

Despite growing resistance on both sides of the border, Díaz attempted to remain in power, but in 1910 this spawned an armed revolt. The ensuing Mexican Revolution would provide a unifying social myth replete with heroes, ultimately giving the rebellion a basis for legitimacy and spawning national ideals. Beginning in 1910, powerful regional caudillos led rebellions throughout Mexico. In May 1911, Díaz, with his army crumbling and rebel victories spreading, resigned his presidency and left Mexico for France. In October 1911, Francisco Madero, a wealthy landowner and caudillo in the northern Mexican state of Coahuila, won election to the presidency.[6] He underestimated the powerful regionalism and caudillismo that existed throughout the country, however, and never gained complete control. He also committed errors in judgment, including releasing from incarceration generals Félix Díaz and Bernardo Reyes, who were in jail for attempting to overthrow his government. Rebellion again broke out in several regions of the country. By 1913, General Victoriano Huerta gained the upper hand among the various rebels and seized the presidency.

While many high-ranking officers of the Mexican army, businesses, and other conservative groups in the country supported Huerta, strong-minded regional caudillos refused to recognize the usurper's position. Governor Venustiano Carranza in Coahuila, Francisco "Pancho" Villa in Chihuahua and Durango, Emiliano Zapata in Morelos, and Alvaro Obregón in Sonora, among others, rebelled against Huerta. In March 1913, leaders in the northern frontier allied under Carranza's Plan de Guadalupe, pledging cooperation to overthrow Huerta and restore constitutional rule. Carranza and his

Francisco Madero, second from left, with his brother Raúl and close associates.
Archivo General de la Nación. México, DF.

followers, calling themselves "Constitutionalists," assumed leadership of the movement to oust Huerta. Carranza, not an army general, took the title of "Primer Jefe" or "First Chief" of this effort. Huerta's political and military strength rapidly deteriorated. Once again, powerful regional caudillos had made it impossible for a government to control the country from Mexico City. In 1914, Huerta resigned and went into exile.[7]

As early as 1913, if not before, Carranza had recognized that if he were to win the battle of the caudillos, he must know what his enemies were doing at all times. Once in a position to monitor enemies of his government, he suggested that the Secretario de Gobernación (Secretariat of Government) be the main civilian agency assigned to securing information related to internal security.[8] He also used the army, both as enforcer of laws and for military intelligence gathering, and the Mexican consuls working within the Secretaría de Relaciones Exteriores (Secretariat of Foreign Relations). In 1914, army leaders established a professional espionage organization within the military that operated independently of civilian agencies. Some of Carranza's supporters suggested the creation of a military system with agents who were well-informed, cosmopolitan, bilingual, and who comported themselves in a sophisticated manner. This plan called for the reports to go directly to the army.[9] Rejecting that approach, the Primer Jefe created that year within Gobernación an agency that became one of the precursors of the Departamento Confidencial. The First Section (Sección Primera), with its chief function the collection of all types of information, also included an Office of Information and Propaganda (Oficina de Información y Propaganda). Once these new agencies were operational, Carranza deployed Sección Primera agents to several important Mexican states as well as to the United States to report upon public opinion and other conditions that might threaten his regime.[10]

Rafael Zubarán Capmany was Carranza's undersecretary of Gobernación and, as such, the initial appointment to the Sección Primera. Carranza was concerned about his enemies, but he also wanted to observe his supporters within and beyond his immediate control.[11] The Primer Jefe and the Mexican army were not alone in the gathering of intelligence, for Francisco "Pancho" Villa and leaders of other factions frequently sent individuals into enemy camps to spy on their activities. Each faction intercepted telegrams, sent agents to report on enemy actions, and listened in on opposition telephone conversations. Individual citizens provided information, while state and central government employees volunteered to spy on colleagues.[12] Few records concerning internal espionage during the carrancista period have surfaced; therefore, what Carranza's efforts accomplished remains unclear. The records that do exist indicate that, until mid-1915, Guilebaldo Nava assumed the task of directing Sección Primera , providing Carranza with a list of individuals within and outside the office of the Secretario de Relaciones Exteriores who could not be trusted. Nava also included comments about threats from within labor movements and other groups in the public sector.[13]

Carranza's espionage activities also involved several women as agents, including Dolores González de Betancourt, who worked in counterespionage during 1916-1917. At approximately the same time, agent J. Soledad Rodríguez collected information concerning the activities of various army officers, who, while serving under command of General Pánfilo Natera, had evidently criticized Carranza.[14] Between June 1915 and March 1916, Jesús Acuña succeeded Nava as director of the Sección Primera [15] Acuña attempted to formalize the structure of the department, asking Carranza to provide funds for a more efficient service. He accomplished little. The Sección Primera finally became a more formal office in 1918, when Carranza authorized the hiring of twenty full-time agents.[16] Despite its reorganization, it had a long way to go before it was professionally administered and fully institutionalized.

Other espionage activities also were occurring in Mexico at this time. During World War I, the United States, England, and Germany dispatched dozens of operatives to the country. These agents engaged in propaganda dissemination and spied on each other as well as Mexico. The United States and Britain enjoyed a wartime advantage over Germany as a consequence of having broken the German diplomatic code. Reading German messages sent to Mexico allowed the Allies to learn almost instantly of the famous Zimmermann Telegram wherein Germany offered Mexico an alliance if it would join against Britain and the United States. According to the telegram, once they defeated the United States, Mexico would be given back its lands lost to its northern neighbor in the previous century, and gain additional territory contiguous to this territory.[17]

By 1915, with Carranza serving as de facto president of Mexico, the war in Europe was raging fiercely, and the Carranza government, through various agencies including the Sección Primera, sought to monitor foreign and local activities that could threaten the security of the country or Carranza's regime. During his presidency, this effort received increasing attention from Gobernación. Displeased with the inefficiency of the espionage effort, Carranza frequently fired his Secretary of Gobernación. When he appointed Lic. Manuel Aguirre Berlanga to the office, he ordered him to replace the directors of the Sección Primera until Berlanga found one who was capable of doing the job. Successively, Rafael Flores, Lamberto García, Jesús Moreno, Miguel Gutiérrez, and General Paulino Navarro served briefly.

Mexican espionage agents also operated in the United States along the international border. The agents collected information among Mexican exiles and monitored the actions of the United States that might impact Mexico. Mexican consuls in the United States, such as Andrés García, whom Carranza appointed in November 1914, were located in El Paso, Texas, and collected information on both sides of the international border. García and other consuls usually recruited and directed activities in their regions and occasionally hired international detective agencies to conduct investigations.

Andrés García, Mexican Consul in El Paso (left); General Alvaro Obregón (center).
Arizona Historical Society, Tucson.

García was especially effective in constructing an intelligence network along the border. His efforts became increasingly valuable as the Carranza regime fought to end the Pancho Villa movement.

In 1915, Carranza changed the way the Sección Primera operated in the United States when he appointed Ramón P. de Negri, Consul General in San Francisco, to reorganize the service, an effort that remained under the consular system until 1916. Determined to restructure substantially its espionage activities in the United States, Negri named Jesús M. Arriola to lead the newly created Mexican Bureau of Investigation, a detective agency that would carry out espionage functions the consul deemed appropriate.[18] Manuel Aguirre Berlanga further transformed intelligence operations under Carranza's leadership, establishing an Agents of the Investigation Service (Servicio de Agentes de Investigaciones) that would eventually evolve into a section of the Departamento Confidencial. Berlanga appointed Aureliano Esquivel as its director, and Esquivel quickly established a few fundamental procedural guidelines for investigations. Over time, more specific guidelines for recruitment and conduct were developed.

Despite Carranza's efforts to stifle the opposition of regional leaders and others opposing his regime, Mexico rapidly fragmented into confused fighting among the various local caudillos who had challenged Huerta, each claiming to be the legitimate heir of the revolutionary movement. April to June 1915 marked a crucial time in this struggle. During this period Carranza's Constitutionalist army, under command of General Alvaro Obregón, defeated Francisco Villa's División del Norte in battles at Celaya and León in Guanajuato, sending Villa and the remnants of his division scurrying northward to safety in the mountains of Durango and Chihuahua.[19] In March 1916, Villa attacked Columbus, New Mexico, on the border between the United States and Mexico, hoping to drag the United States into battles against Carranza. President Woodrow Wilson dispatched General John J. Pershing and approximately ten thousand soldiers to apprehend Villa in what became known as the "Punitive Expedition." Some of the troops patrolled the international border, while approximately six thousand entered Mexico to capture Villa. The expedition was unsuccessful. By February 1917, with the United States preparing to enter World War I, Wilson decided that the Carranza government could deal with Villa more effectively. Pershing and his

General Francisco (Pancho) Villa and his Dorados, 1914-1915.
Archivo General de la Nación. México, DF.

Constitutionalist Soldiers in Chihuahua, 1916-1918.
Archivo General de la Nación. México, DF.

General Benjamin Hill, leading the Constitutionalist army against Pancho Villa, 1915.
Archivo General de la Nación. México, DF.

Villista troops fleeing the Constitutionalist army, 1915-1916.
Archivo General de la Nación. México, DF.

President Venustiano Carranza (fourth from left) with his generals.
General Plutarco Elías Calles is on the front row, far left.
Archivo General de la Nación. México, DF.

troops returned to the United States to prepare for the European war that had been raging since 1914.

Carranza continued his quest to control the country after United States troops departed. By 1917, he had achieved a measure of success over several of his major regional foes.[20] Furthermore, through various means he gained considerable control over state officials, especially in the northern and northeastern sections of the country. Governors, many of whom also were military officers, expected the Carranza regime to send military supplies, funds, and troops to help defend their regions from antigovernment forces or from the United States. Carranza did his best to deliver on their expectations, thereby tying these regional caudillos to his government. In turn, the caudillos generally bowed to Carranza's requests or orders, clearly indicating that at least temporarily he had established a degree of central government authority in the country.[21]

That year he called a constituent congress in Querétaro, where political and military leaders from various sections of the country wrote a new constitution. The resulting Constitution of 1917 established the framework of a government that has endured into the twenty-first century. Elected as president in 1917, Carranza sought to stabilize the country, centralize power, and continue modernization begun during the Díaz regime. In April 1919, the carrancista government eliminated Emiliano Zapata, a champion of the rural poor and a local leader. Other individuals and groups, both in Mexico City and in outlying regions, continued to oppose Carranza. The Primer Jefe understood the threat to his regime posed by caudillismo and regionalism. Throughout his efforts to bring stability to Mexico, Carranza remained concerned about internal centrifugal forces—the problems created as a consequence of the country's vast size, regional differences, and the historic difficulty of controlling the nation from Mexico City.

As the election of 1920 approached, Carranza was unwilling to relinquish his authority and sought to keep the government out of the hands of the military. The caudillo General Alvaro Obregón, the brilliant Sonoran military leader in the revolutionary fighting, had returned temporarily to his farming operations. It soon became obvious to Carranza that he intended to offer himself as a candidate for the presidency in the election of 1920. In April of that year, as a consequence of Carranza's persistent attempts to thrust his close friend Ignacio Bonillas into the presidency, an armed revolt against the government quickly spread throughout the country. Three days later, the leaders of the rebellion in Sonora—Generals Obregón, Plutarco Elías Calles, and Adolfo de la Huerta—issued the Plan de Agua Prieta, withdrawing recognition from the Carranza government and explaining that they opposed his continuing control over the presidency. On May 7, 1920, with opposition forces closing in on Mexico City, Carranza departed for Veracruz aboard a train carrying his archives and most of the government treasury. Opposition troops soon blocked Carranza's escape by stopping the train on which he was riding. Carranza and some cohorts set out on horseback across the state of Puebla to escape. They stopped at the mountain village of Tlaxcalantongo, where during the night Carranza was murdered. The rebellion against Carranza was the last successful military uprising against a presidential election. The later revolts of 1923, 1927, and 1938 failed to gain sufficient support to destabilize the government. Throughout the period after 1920, the military slowly professionalized and its influence declined.

With Carranza dead, disagreement arose between Obregón supporters and those who opposed him for the presidency. Factions were specifically contesting who would be interim president of Mexico until the election later that year. After some wrangling among leading caudillos, General Adolfo de la Huerta emerged victorious. Sworn in as interim president on June 1, 1920, he would serve until a new president could be elected. He occupied the presidency for six months, during which time his major accomplishment was to arrive at a peace settlement with Pancho Villa, effectively retiring the northern revolutionary leader. De la Huerta also invited expatriates to return to Mexico, resolved governing problems in Baja California, and generally encouraged a spirit of cooperation among regional caudillos, revolutionary factions, and the national government.

In December 1920, General Obregón, having won the election, assumed the presidency and appointed General Plutarco Elías Calles as Secretary of Gobernación. For the next fourteen years, one or the other of these two men dominated Mexican politics, whether in the presidency or not. It was during this era that the central government established the Departamento Confidencial, the agency that conducted internal espionage after 1920. It soon became a useful service for the government as it gathered a great variety of social and political information.

Venustiano Carranza (second from right, wearing a bowler) and supporters, ca. 1919-1920.
Archivo General de la Nación, México, DF.

CHAPTER 2

EL DEPARTAMENTO CONFIDENCIAL, 1920–1930

General Alvaro Obregón was elected to the presidency on September 5, 1920, and began his four-year term in December. An experienced military leader born in Sonora near the port of Guaymas, Obregón realized that Mexico would be difficult to govern, a challenge rising from the previous decade of revolutionary fighting and the strong regionalism pervading the country.[1] Mexico's economy was in shambles, sporadic revolutionary fighting persisted, and political conditions remained chaotic. Due to Sonora's isolation and considerable distance from Mexico City, and because of the leader's experience as a farmer and businessman, Obregón understood the problems the national government faced in bringing such areas under its control.[2] He further realized that, to stabilize the country, sufficient political and military power must be vested in the central government to override the decentralizing tendencies that characterized local caudillo rule. Obregón brought a level of decisiveness and understanding to the presidency that was rare in the history of Mexican politics. He believed that centralization of authority was necessary to create political and social conditions that would promote material progress, a critical need in Mexico after revolutionary fighting had ceased. Upon assuming the presidency, his immediate concern was stabilizing the country politically and improving economic and social opportunities. As Linda B. Hall has written, Obregón was popular with the majority of Mexicans, and this played a significant role in his ability to reestablish "political institutions and political stability."[3]

In order to win the presidency, Obregón had favored and used labor organizations, most specifically the Regional Confederation of Mexican Workers (Confederación Regional Obrera Mexicana, or CROM). Luis N. Morones, the leader of this group, recognized that an opportunity existed to improve labor conditions and increase his personal power if he cooperated with Obregón. By the middle 1920s, Morones led more than one million

General Alvaro Obregón as president.
Fideicomiso Archivos Plutarco Elías Calles y Fernando Torreblanca. México, DF.

workers. In return for Morones's support, the Obregón government subsidized CROM and helped Morones stop radical labor groups from gaining a foothold among Mexican workers.

Obregón also favored some aspects of agrarian reform for the peasants of rural Mexico, but he preferred moderation in land policies and, according to many reformers, moved too slowly to increase land distribution and create an agrarian system as outlined in the Constitution of 1917. Specifically, he did not, to any significant degree, confiscate the lands of hacendados and redistribute them to peasants. Opposition developed from organizations on both sides of the political spectrum. Those on the radical left, such as the Communists, so agitated the president that he deported many of their foreign leaders. Obregón also reacted negatively toward the country's conservative Catholic organizations, although it would be his successor, General Plutarco Elías Calles, who saw the Catholic Church as the source of many of the country's problems. Conservative Catholic organizations reacted against Obregón through street demonstrations and later against Calles by armed rebellion.

Once securely in power, Obregón named his fellow Sonoran and loyal friend, General Calles, to the ever more influential position of Secretario de Gobernación, a position second only to the presidency in influence and power in the country. Calles agreed with what Obregón wished to accomplish in respect to political centralization, stability, and material progress even if the two men differed in their methods and attitudes toward democracy and the Catholic Church. As Jürgen Buchenau has written, Calles "displayed little interest in representative democracy, which had failed in the nineteenth century and, again, in the Revolution. He disdained popular participation in politics and regarded regional and local differences as evidence of chaos."[4]

Calles was aware of the internal monitoring of politics and society before 1920 and intended to strengthen internal espionage operations. Once ensconced in Gobernación, he contributed significantly to Obregón's efforts to centralize authority. Calles could now deploy all the tools of the national government to accomplish his ends, and he was determined to employ an internal agency that monitored political and social activities as one method of centralizing power. After 1920, Calles created the Departamento Confidencial (Confidential Department) from the remnants of similar agencies that Carranza had employed. With marginally adequate financing, Calles was able to hire only a few agents. As finances allowed, these operatives traveled throughout the country, later submitting written reports to the agency. Under Calles's leadership, internal monitoring of all things political and social ultimately became an institutionalized activity.

Initially, the Departamento Confidencial was inefficient, although it slowly improved the quality of its agents and its methods. Making matters more difficult, agents received only irregular technical training to improve information gathering. Calles was determined to improve the operation. He was aware that some agents were not objective in their reports; others did not have the training or ability to write clearly. During the agency's formative period, its investigators did not complete assignments quickly enough for the information to get to Calles in a timely manner. In addition to these problems, the agency had no permanent office until Calles eventually provided for its location, on Bucareli street in Mexico City.[5] During 1923, Calles's most worthwhile revision was the establishment of an archive for the office, which allowed it to keep relatively good records of its activities. (This archive formed the beginning of the records of the Departamento Confidencial in what is now called the Dirección General de Investigaciones Políticas y Sociales (DGIPS) collection presently housed in the Mexican National Archives (Archivo General de la Nación.) Agents submitted their reports to the director who read them and decided what information to file in the archives and what to pass on to the office of the president. Office staff filed the reports according to topics or the types of agent activities. Occasionally, the director wrote a note in the margin of a report and asked the agent for clarification before filing the information. By 1924, Calles had created an improved and better-financed internal monitoring agency.

Obregón's presidency did not begin or end without conflict. Political instability during the previous violent era, and Mexico's refusal to allow unregulated drilling for oil, had led the United States to withhold official recognition of Mexico's governments. Additionally, opposition to Obregón from within the country sparked considerable internal conflict. The need for significant agrarian reform combined with an economic recession posed serious problems for the Sonoran caudillo. Land ownership remained in the hands of the great hacendados, and the landless poor across the country echoed the heirs of Emiliano Zapata, clamoring loudly for the redistribution of some of these holdings. The banking system was also in chaos. Difficulties with the United States centered upon property rights, particularly oil ownership rights, and back taxes foreign oil companies owed the Mexican government. By early 1923, international oil difficulties were less volatile, and Mexico tentatively agreed not to seize oil company assets. The two countries soon normalized diplomatic relations after the United States extended diplomatic recognition to Mexico.

There is no documentary evidence that Calles's creation of the Departamento Confidencial late in 1922 occurred as a consequence of conflicts with the United States. Nevertheless, agents worked extensively in Veracruz and along the United States–Mexico border. In their reports they included information about the activities of foreign companies, including many based in the United States.

By the end of 1923, former president and Sonoran caudillo Adolfo de la Huerta, still influential in Mexican politics, charged that Obregón's agreements with the United States were demeaning to Mexico. He also believed they could be a violation of the principles of the Constitution of 1917. He was not alone in this criticism, and many other regionally powerful caudillos also opposed the settlement. By late 1923, the question of presidential succession further complicated the political stability of Mexico. De la Huerta desired to return to the presidency, but Obregón supported his close friend General Calles.

De la Huerta hesitated to rebel against fellow Sonoran Obregón, but ultimately, at Veracruz on December 7, 1923, he signed a document that placed him at the head of a revolt against the government.[6] Joining this rebellion were generals Fortunato Maycotte, Enrique Estrada, Guadalupe Sánchez, and Manuel M. Diéguez, among other influential regional caudillos who commanded troops in various regions of the country. Obregón enjoyed support from generals Joaquín Amaro, Eugenio Martínez, Francisco Serrano, Vicente González, Lázaro Cárdenas, Juan Andreu Almazán, and other regionally powerful military and civilian leaders. As the threats to his regime spread to several sections of the country, Obregón left the capital for Guanajuato, where he personally directed his military operations. The de la Huerta revolt suffered setbacks throughout the country. In March 1924, de

General Francisco (Pancho) Villa, fourth from left, with some of his troops.
Archivo General de la Nación. México, DF.

la Huerta realized that he could not stop the succession of Calles; therefore, he fled Mexico, traveling first to Cuba and then to the United States. He had hoped to secure support from the United States, but was unsuccessful, and by the middle of 1924 the Mexican government had defeated the rebellion. Government troops caught and executed several of the opposing generals. The work of agents of the Departamento Confidencial led officials to the area where these rebels were hiding and informed the government of existing local support, but no evidence exists that a specific investigation led to any individual's capture or elimination. Obregón returned to Mexico City to orchestrate Calles's ascendancy to the presidency. De la Huerta remained in the United States, settling in California.

Further complicating politics during late 1923, Pancho Villa emerged as a potential political candidate for the election of 1924. That was enough to prompt his execution, which took place as he drove out of Parral, Chihuahua, one afternoon after a night of merriment with a few of his guards. It has remained somewhat unclear who was responsible, but recent research has suggested that Obregón and Calles were behind his murder. Both had opposed making any deals with Villa when de la Huerta had negotiated with

Pancho Villa in death, July 1923.
Universidad Nacional Autónoma de México, DF.

the northern caudillo. No documents in the files of the Departamento Confidencial mention Villa. If any agent reports existed, they were eliminated.

In December 1924, Calles assumed the presidency of Mexico and set about consolidating and centralizing power in the Distrito Federal. He was determined to use all governmental powers at his disposal to accomplish this. Historian Jürgen Buchenau has referred to Calles as an "authoritarian populist" who believed it necessary "to use force as he deemed appropriate."[7] There were several reasons for Calles's attitudes. In 1906, Calles had witnessed considerable violence in the Cananea miners' strike in Sonora and decided he could not accept this kind of societal disorder. In fact, he had earlier cooperated with the Porfirian authorities in an effort to protect political stability, and he was a late advocate of the movement to overthrow Díaz. Furthermore, Buchenau has suggested that Calles "deprecated representative democracy as a naive sham. Like the científicos whose positivist philosophy had educated him, he viewed politics as administration, and he was far more interested in the outcome than in the process of politics."[8]

Prior conflicts with the Catholic Church and with other regional caudillos continued into Calles's presidency. Throughout this period it became evident

General Plutarco Elías Calles, newly elected President of México.
Fideicomiso Archivos Plutarco Elías Calles y Fernando Torreblanca. México, DF.

to Calles which groups and individuals supported him and which could not be trusted. Morones continued his support for Calles, and during his presidency Calles supported the CROM, the labor organization Morones led. After he became president, Calles rewarded Morones for his loyalty, naming him secretary of labor. The powerful labor leader and his organization profited immensely as a consequence of Calles's support, and membership increased to more than two million by 1928. During the Obregón administration and early in his presidency, Calles also promoted Joaquín de la Peña, a future director of the Departamento Confidencial. A native of Querétaro, de la Peña had sought to win the governorship of his home state. Failing at this attempt, he worked closely with Calles to defy any government opposition emerging within the region. In 1924, he notified Calles that political leaders in Querétaro who had promised to support him were, in fact, plotting against him. Once he became president, Calles appointed de la Peña to general officer rank in the army as a reward for his loyalty.[9]

Calles believed that recurring rebellions against the government clearly demonstrated the importance of knowing the social and political conditions in the country. As Obregón's most faithful supporter, and Secretario de Gobernación, Calles was in a position to use the powers of government, specifically those concentrated in the Departamento Confidencial, to monitor the activities of those who were not completely committed to Obregón or to him. During Obregón's presidency and in his own, Calles reorganized and strengthened the Departamento Confidencial. While he was Secretario de Gobernación, Calles appointed Gilberto Valenzuela, a civilian, to direct

Antigovernment rebels being executed, ca. 1920-1930.
Archivo General de la Nación. México, DF.

activities, his loyalty to Calles fulfilling the leader's preeminent qualifica-
tion for the position. In the year following Valenzuela's appointment, Calles
oversaw many administrative changes within the agency. In 1923, for example,
agents were renamed First Class Confidential Agents (Agentes Confidenciales
de Primera) and Second Class Confidential Agents (Agentes Confidenciales de
Segunda). The former received fifteen pesos per day plus expenses, as before,
and the latter were paid twelve pesos daily, along with expenses. By the
end of 1923, C. C. Rafael Flores, Lamberto García, Jesús Moreno, Miguel
Gutiérrez, and Paulino Navarro, who died in December 1923, had served
as chiefs of the agency.[10] All had served previously in similar positions under Carranza. Calles offered no public explanation for these changes in
leadership.

By establishing a hierarchy among agents and formalizing their pay
scale, Calles was able to improve the operation of the Departamento Confidencial under Obregón's administration. While Calles was occupied alongside Obregón in suppressing military revolts, he nonetheless continued to
expand and enhance the department so that it became an asset to him and
the president. Its structure, however, remained incomplete until 1924. In
December of that year, Calles, finally in office as president, began to use the
department entirely for his own ends. Under Obregón's presidency, Calles
had already been appointing the chiefs of the agency. Between January 1,
1924, and January 11, 1925, under the direction of Martín F. Bárcenas, a
stalwart supporter of Obregón and Calles who had replaced Navarro upon
his death the previous year, the Departamento Confidencial underwent one
of its many name changes. During this period, the agency was transformed
and officially renamed the Confidential Department, Office of Political and
Social Investigations (Departamento Confidencial, Oficina de Investigaciones Políticas y Sociales).

Upon his appointment in December 1924, Bárcenas suggested that
Calles reorganize the agency, insisting that, in Mexico, the department had
not received the attention that such a service enjoyed in other countries.
He further suggested that the department act more vigorously to identify
people and factions who supported Obregón and Calles, though he maintained it was even more important to determine which of the many political
and social groups in the country were not faithful to the regime. According

to Bárcenas, the department needed to augment its activities among civilians by forming a political and administrative division. He believed that political problems in the various states often did not come to the attention of the central government until they were almost too serious to resolve. He suggested that it might be a more efficient operation if an agent of the department was stationed permanently in each state where the agent could monitor the daily activities of state officials. Calles was sympathetic to the idea, but there were too few agents and too little funding to accomplish his proposal. Bárcenas also believed that public officials frequently defrauded the people, the national government, and the state by stealing money and land. He informed Calles that some members of the police force in the Distrito Federal were protecting drug dealers and receiving a share of the proceeds in return. To counter this larceny, Bárcenas suggested to Calles that agents should gather more information on public officials, noting that the identity of the agents must always be protected for their safety.[11]

There were only twenty agents on the payroll when Bárcenas assumed control of the department in January 1924. However, because he was frequently away from the office, sometimes for extended periods, his subchief, Lt. Col. Ignacio Jiménez, actually directed the department until August 11, when Gobernación relieved him. (In 1931, Jiménez reappeared in this department as an agent, but General Lázaro Cárdenas, then Secretary of Gobernación, also fired him. A short time later, police shot and killed Jiménez at the Hotel Regis, not far from the center of the Distrito Federal. His killing may have been related to information sent to his chief in Gobernación, but no documents exist to substantiate this.)

While Bárcenas was otherwise occupied, often away coordinating agency efforts to end the de la Huerta rebellion, Jiménez and others made significant changes in the procedures of the department. Jiménez altered how the agents conducted investigations and how quickly they performed their tasks. He insisted upon more complete documentation of departmental investigations, held agents reporting to work to strict schedules, established rules and guidelines to assure that agents provided valid information, and in essence established the structure that transformed the department into a true intelligence operation. Finally, he reorganized the agency's archive with a document numbering system so information could be stored and retrieved easily from an index.

In August 1924, temporary chief Lt. Col. Eufrasio Ortega assumed control of the Departamento Confidencial. On January 11, 1925, he officially became the director, and Bárcenas eventually moved on to become Inspector of Police in the Distrito Federal. It is unclear whether or not this appointment came because he exposed police corruption; perhaps Bárcenas himself had become part of the corrupt system. Whatever the circumstance, no other directors of the Departamento Confidencial commented on the police and drug connection during this period. It is also worth noting that while the department collected information about individuals who were eventually assassinated, no extant document directly ties the agency to these killings.

Ortega brought additional reorganization to the Departamento Confidencial, and further improved investigation processes and agent conduct; he also demanded that agents submit accurate and clearly written reports. Furthermore, Ortega reiterated that agents were not to disclose to their friends or family that they worked for the department. It was he, too, who provided identification cards for the agents, identifying them as newspaper reporters and travel agents. Ortega further modernized the department when he purchased a photostatic copy machine to copy documents.

During 1925–1926, the department continued to undergo changes. Significantly, it embarked upon investigations into the background of political candidates who sought positions as deputies and senators to the national congress. In terms of day-to-day operations, directors of the agency reemphasized existing guidelines and established new ones for the department and its agents. For example, the chief of the department ordered agents to use the telegraph system for communication whenever possible, and they were instructed to have telephones installed in their homes if they had none. Written communications were to be submitted in triplicate. For security reasons, no strangers would be admitted to the offices of the department. Moreover, the agency conducted classes for its agents between 7:00 and 8:30 in the morning. In these meetings agents received instruction in the history of Mexico and the political affairs of various states. The aim was for agents to understand the political situation in the country and learn how to conduct investigations in secret. Agents were told to be discreet, treat people properly, be diligent in their work, read the newspapers in order to be informed about public issues, and obey the orders of superiors. Agents were each assigned a number that they were to use in place of their names; their real identities were to remain secret. If operating undercover, the agent's automobile might be assigned police license plates.

Throughout this period, the Departamento Confidencial continued to reimburse agents for their expenses, but they had to document these expenditures carefully. As it was earlier in the history of the department, some agents who served during this period were classified as Agentes Confidenciales de Primera and received fifteen pesos daily in salary and ten pesos daily for expenses. Meanwhile, Agentes Confidenciales de Segunda received twelve pesos daily in salary and eight pesos for expenses, and a new class, called Agentes Confidenciales de Tercera (Third Class Confidential Agents), received even lower pay and reimbursement. (The salaries and expenses paid occasionally fluctuated during this period.) There were two additional types of agents at this time, including Information Agents (Agentes de Información), who investigated undercover, and Executive or Detective Agents (Agentes Ejecutores or Policíacos), who carried legitimate identification cards and performed police duties on behalf of the agency. Each day between 7:00 and 8:00 in the morning, the head of the department received a report from all operatives. In situations considered urgent, the director usually made assignments by telephone; otherwise he directed agents to come into the office.

Ortega resigned on May 11, 1925, and Gilberto Valenzuela, secretary of Gobernación under Calles at this time, appointed Col. Francisco M. Delgado as chief of the department. Delgado was a dedicated public servant, and extremely loyal to Calles, which likely contributed to his appointment. Originally from Guanajuato, Delgado was educated, cultured, and a former colonel in the Constitutionalist army during the revolutionary fighting. He served as chief between 1925 and 1930 for all but a few brief intervals.

Delgado treated his agents well, and the department flourished under his leadership. Immediately upon assuming his position, he sought to professionalize the agency. His administrative revisions improved agency operations and established a long-term plan for strengthening its influence. One of the first things on Delgado's agenda was to tighten security in respect to the identity of the agents. Similar action had been taken in the past, but he wanted to reinforce among agents the confidential nature of their work. He instructed all employees to deny any knowledge when asked if they or anyone else worked for the department. During much of this time, while the chief of the department was out of town or dealing with other government business, the assistant chief (subjefe) directed the department. In 1926, the Secretario de Gobernación renamed the agency temporarily, calling it the Confidential Office (Oficina Confidencial), a name that lasted only until January 1, 1928, when it again became the Departamento Confidencial.

During the power struggles of the early 1920s, the activities of the Departamento Confidencial in Jalisco offer insight into how the agents operated in the field.[12] In that state, General Enrique Estrada, commanding the Second Division of federal troops, joined the de la Huerta rebellion, but local caudillo José Guadalupe Zuno did not take a firm stand. Zuno was antichurch and anti-central government, strongly supporting local control. Zuno sought support from laborers and campesinos in Jalisco and opposed Luis Morones, who as leader of CROM supported Calles. Zuno believed that Morones and his organization posed a great threat to his local influence. The primary reason for his concern was that Morones sought to bring regional workers under his control; for this reason, Zuno feared the locals would more likely do Morones's bidding than his own. In fact, Zuno had warrant for his concern, for Morones was gradually expanding his influence within all states of the Republic in preparation for a future bid for the presidency.

On March 10, 1923, Zuno forced Governor Basilio Vadillo from office, concerned that the governor would not only oppose him, but might support Calles and the central government in any confrontation between Zuno and Calles. Zuno then assumed the position of governor of the state. His ascendancy did not inaugurate radicalism, despite his socialistic and anticlerical ranting. He was primarily concerned with holding his position and maintaining freedom of action without regard to the national government. In this respect, Zuno was just the type of regional caudillo the central government had long struggled to control. He was, however, so much less conservative and Catholic than most of his constituents that he soon found himself in conflict with various groups. For example, he had attempted to keep local army leader General Enrique Estrada neutral in the de la Huerta rebellion, but had been unsuccessful.[13]

By this time, Obregón realized that Zuno posed a threat to the national government. Acting on Obregón's behalf, Calles dispatched an agent of the

President Calles (center left, with hand in pocket) at a construction site.
Fideicomiso Archivos Plutarco Elías Calles y Fernando Torreblanca. México, DF.

Departamento Confidencial to monitor Zuno's activities. The agent reported that it was General Estrada who had supported de la Huerta during the rebellion. In fact, Zuno had been forced to flee when Estrada led his troops into Guadalajara. Zuno again occupied the governorship when federal troops finally evicted Estrada's army from Guadalajara early in 1924, whereupon Zuno sought to punish the pro-rebellion factions. He also acted against the Catholic Church, but only after the Church had confirmed his young daughter, the future wife of former president Luis Echeverría Álvarez. He confiscated church property and closed monasteries, schools, and orphanages.[14]

Then in March 1926 Zuno resigned the governorship to become a candidate for election to the national Cámara de Diputados (Chamber of Deputies). A few days later he spoke to a gathering of his supporters, where he insisted that all his actions as governor had been in support of the principles set forth in the Constitution of 1917, a document he said was profoundly federal in form and one that respected local sovereignty. The crowd welcomed him enthusiastically, whereupon he launched into a tirade against the conservatives in Jalisco and the "capitalism of the Yankees" as the cause of most problems in Jalisco. He told the excited crowd that he hoped that they would not be "seduced by the false promises of CROM," reminding them that the central government's policies had caused most of their suffering. In the crowd gathered around Zuno was agent Sánchez Aldama, who took careful notes about what Zuno said and immediately sent the information to Mexico City.[15] The agent also reported that he talked with some of the workers at the meeting, and they all agreed that Zuno was the only person who "understood the needs of the campesinos and laborers of Jalisco." To help communicate the extent of Zuno's popularity to his superiors, the agent made a list of the important local leaders who had spoken with Zuno following the speech. The agent further expressed the belief that Zuno orchestrated a miner's strike in Jalisco shortly after this gathering.[16] Finally, the agent advised his department that enemies of the government were likely reading the messages he telegraphed to Mexico City, and he needed a code system to assure the confidentiality of his communications. Agent Sánchez Aldama remained in Guadalajara for several months collecting information about potential or actual antigovernment activities.[17] Despite such intelligence, Zuno remained the local power broker for decades, a persistent thorn in the side of the national government.

As chief of the Departamento Confidencial, Francisco M. Delgado occasionally worked in the field, and often, upon Calles's orders, sent agents to the United States–Mexico border. Mexican police, working with Departamento Confidencial operatives along the northern international border, received threats and found themselves in dangerous situations resulting from confrontations with local Texas authorities. An incident in 1926 illustrates the attitudes of Texas lawmen, if not of the entire United States, toward Mexican operatives. The incident was recorded by two agents who, later that year, traveled to Nuevo Laredo to investigate antigovernment activities on both sides. Eventually, they crossed the border to Laredo, Texas, where they followed leads about antigovernment activities of both the Catholic Church and de la Huerta loyalists, who had continued to pursue de la Huerta's conservative goals, even after his exile to the United States. While in Laredo, these Departamento Confidencial operatives heard about the plight of an agent of the Mexican Federal District Police, Eusebio Izquierdo, whom Texas authorities had jailed.

According to these agents' reports, on February 6, 1926, Izquierdo had entered the United States to talk with the sheriff of Webb County, Texas, about border matters. According to Texas authorities, agent Izquierdo had his pistol on his hip, carrying it illegally north of the border. At the Laredo county courthouse, he went to see the sheriff whom he had met previously. When Izquierdo arrived, the sheriff was talking with county prosecutor John Valls. Upon seeing him, the sheriff said "hello" in Spanish and then spoke to Valls in English. The two men asked Izquierdo to come to the sheriff's office, where the prosecutor asked him why he had brought a pistol into the United States. Izquierdo said he had done so under a special permission signed by Gus T. Jones, a United States Department of Justice official, and by Captain William Hanson, Chief of the United States Department of Immigration. At that point the sheriff confiscated the pistol and said that he believed that Izquierdo had entered the United States to assassinate General Lucio Blanco, who had fled the Calles regime. Izquierdo protested that he was no assassin, claiming that several United States officials in San Antonio could vouch for him. Valls answered angrily, "Ni que Jones ni la chingada a todos los hacen pendejos, para mí no." (While this expression resists literal translation, it means, roughly, that Valls did not care what Jones or "any other son-of-a-bitch" or "prick" had to say.) Valls then asked to call the Mexican consul, whereupon the prosecutor told him that the consul was not worth a damn. When Izquierdo continued to protest, Valls replied, "Shut up you son-of-a-bitch." The affair was resolved after the two Departamento agents paid Izquierdo's $250 fine. Izquierdo reported to his government that the county prosecutor put the money in his pocket.[18]

During the Calles presidency, agents of the Departamento Confidencial also scrutinized the activities of various labor organizations. On January 24, 1926, the local council of the Confederation of Railroad Societies of the Mexican Republic (Confederación de Sociedades Ferrocarrileras de la República Mexicana) invited all labor organizations that had anything to do with railroads to meet at the Cine Mina (Mina Theater) in Mexico City for a forum on government and labor problems. A dozen speakers from the groups took the podium before an audience of more than three hundred workers. Among them was an agent of the Departamento Confidencial, who observed and noted what was said and recorded the audience reaction. He then presented his interpretation of the events to his superiors. The first speaker, a representative of the Mechanics' Union, claimed that some workers wanted to place the group under the control of Luis Morones, who wished to make the group an instrument of his personal ambitions. A second speaker from the group, not originally on the program, said he did not have the oratorical skills to make his argument widely known, but he insisted that the CROM had ceased to become a social institution, as it was originally intended, and had instead become a political one that sought to make Luis Morones the next president of Mexico. The agent listened carefully to this message and that of a speaker named Camarillo, who argued that the railroad group had three powerful enemies: CROM, the government, and the railroad companies. He suggested that the workers strike to see if the government "with all its bayonets and fifty thousand drunks could run the railroads."[19]

Similar gatherings occurred in many sections of the country as Morones attempted to consolidate his power through his organization. In many respects, these activities ran parallel to the power struggles between the national government and regional strongmen. Although Morones's success with CROM would usher in more central control, increasing Morones's personal power was obviously not in Calles's best interest. Calles understood

President Calles, hand in pocket, awaits the arrival of General Obregón with Luis Morones (in white suit), among others.
Fideicomiso Archivos Plutarco Elías Calles y Fernando Torreblanca. México, DF.

this, however, and sought to use Morones for his own ends, as a means of controlling the country from the Mexican capital.

During Calles's presidency, additional problems arose throughout the country. Calles sought to implement the anticlerical provisions of the constitution, prompting Catholic Church leaders in the country to challenge his actions. In 1926, the Catholic Church rejected Calles's efforts to limit property ownership of the church and his meddling in internal matters related to the expulsion of foreign-born priests. Clergy rebelled and suspended church functions, refusing to say mass or perform baptisms, marriages, and other rites. By the end of 1926, these protests evolved into armed rebellion against the government as religious devotees across the country took up arms in what became known as the Cristero Rebellion. The Cristero movement was pro-Catholic and militant, and the conflict continued until 1929, when both sides moderated their positions. Calles used every means at his disposal to contain this rebellion, including sending agents of the Departamento Confidencial to spy on church activities.

As with Morones and CROM, the church-state battle was about money, power, and influence. Calles viewed the Catholic Church as a threat to state sovereignty. As a consequence of its wealth, and because of its influence in

Front row, left to right: President Calles, US labor leader Samuel Gompers, General Obregón, Luis Morones.
Fideicomiso Archivos Plutarco Elías Calles y Fernando Torreblanca. México, DF.

rural regions, especially among agrarian workers and the poor, Calles considered the church a threat to him and to the process of building a modern nation. He said that the Catholic Church, both past and present, acted as if it were above the laws of secular government.

Typical of the activities of the Departamento Confidencial in respect to the Catholic Church was a scenario involving three agents who were sent to a small store in the San Cosme district of Mexico City, which reportedly harbored a large quantity of religious items. Probably at Calles's request—Calles and Delgado worked closely on all matters—Delgado sent agents to close the store and report their findings to the department. Five days later the agents reported that they had found "ten boxes containing religious books [and] six boxes wherein they found six candle holders or candelabro," along with many other religious artifacts. They closed the store and confiscated religious items they deemed dangerous to public welfare. There was no mention of how they made this determination.[20] In another house in Mexico City, agents discovered an altar, religious ornaments, and priestly attire. They learned that a religious tract was published at the house and interviewed the neighbors, who speculated about strange religious ceremonies they claimed were held there.[21]

Captured weapons of the Cristero rebels, ca. 1928.
Fideicomiso Archivos Plutarco Elías Calles y Fernando Torreblanca. México, DF.

In September 1928, agents of the Departamento Confidencial returned to Guadalajara to compile information about the Cristeros and others opposing the government. Agent Emilio Zurita did not send a report immediately to Delgado, for Zurita was having trouble learning the departmental code system. He also told Delgado that he was concerned about expenses, claiming that he had been buying drinks in a local bar to loosen tongues. Zurita informed his superiors that all of this bar patronage was entirely business, that he personally was "almost an enemy of alcohol," and that he imbibed only when forced to do so to obtain information. Zurita also sent information about local political campaigning, religious gatherings, and army troop movements in Jalisco.[22]

Zurita frequently submitted detailed reports to his department along with analyses of the locations he visited in a particular state. He traveled widely in the state where he was working, talking to many individuals who seemed favorable toward the government. In respect to the army, he reported that it demonstrated almost no activity against rebels in Jalisco and that, for the most part, the troops remained in their garrisons, blaming muddy and impassible roads for their inactivity. When rebels killed a municipal president, regional army commander General Andrés Figueroa finally led five hundred troops out of their garrison in pursuit. Agent Zurita admitted that the government troops operated under very severe conditions, for most of the people in the state were fanatical Catholic believers who shouted "Viva Cristo Rey" whenever soldiers passed by. In Zurita's opinion, the state was infested with antigovernment rebels who apparently operated without allegiance to any particular leader.[23]

As the presidential election of 1928 approached, Calles faced additional political problems. He and Obregón had previously negotiated an agreement that once Calles had served his term, Obregón would return to the presidency. Calles and Obregón believed that laws Congress passed during 1926 permitted *non*consecutive reelection. During the same period Congress had also lengthened the presidential term to six years. In 1927, however, individuals who supported the original no-reelection provisions of the Constitution of 1917 actively opposed Obregón's return to the presidency. Antireeleccionistas, as they became known, rapidly organized and persuaded several prominent army generals, including Francisco R. Serrano and Arnulfo R.

Cristeros and their dead.
Fideicomiso Archivos Plutarco Elías Calles y Fernando Torreblanca. México, DF.

Mexican soldiers on the frontier, 1929.
Arizona Historical Society, Tucson.

Gómez, to join the movement. Both had considerable army support and be-lieved they should be the next president, although Gómez had more support in the important regions of the country.

As the reelection conflict escalated, Gómez campaigned vigorously around the country, as did Obregón. After armed rebellion broke out, but before much fighting erupted, Calles, with Obregón and General Joaquín Amaro at his side, ordered the capture of Serrano and his immediate sup-porters. Soon thereafter, loyal government troops captured and executed fourteen men, including General Serrano. Gómez suffered a similar fate in early November. Obregonistas subsequently used the threat of continued violence as pretext to arrest or eliminate antireeleccionistas they considered potentially dangerous. Most of these individuals had no part in the rebellion. On July 1, 1928, Obregón was reelected for a six-year term. The antireelec tion movement did not end at this time, however, and a hard-core group of antireelection supporters continued to plan for the next confrontation with any government wishing to place a former president back into office. For example, in 1932 several antireeleccionista state governors met multiple times to consider a strategy to follow when it became necessary. Agents of the Departamento Confidencial either infiltrated the meetings or were privy to what occurred and reported their findings to headquarters.[24]

Although Obregón had supported Calles against the Cristeros, he lost any opportunity to resolve the issue soon after his reelection. In the middle of July, at a banquet held in the president-elect's honor, José de León Toral, an itinerant artist and devoted Cristero, fired several shots into Obregón's face, killing him instantly. With Obregón dead, Calles faced considerable difficulties as he attempted to shape Mexico's immediate future. By September he managed to reassert his influence, supporting Emilio Portes Gil to become provisional president for the next fourteen months. Calles's choice of Portes Gil sparked further revolt over presidential succession and terms. On March 3, 1929, a number of commanding generals in different regions of the country, cooperating with several important civilians, launched a revolt against Calles and his choice for provisional president. Meeting at Hermosillo, Sonora, dissidents proclaimed the Plan de Hermosillo, supporting General José Gonzalo Escobar, military commander in Coahuila, as leader of the military revolt. The revolt was focused largely in the north, although a few generals in other parts of the country joined the insurgents. Portes Gil asked Calles to assume the position of Minister of War and Navy to put down the rebellion. By the middle of April, government troops, including those led by Generals Lázaro Cárdenas and Juan Andreu Almazán, had defeated the uprising. Surviving rebels fled to the United States. Satisfied that state matters were as he wished, Calles resigned his position and returned to private life. That move, however, was primarily cosmetic.

Calles had planned all along to find a mechanism beyond the Departamento Confidencial to help him centralize authority and to monitor political and social conditions in the country after he left the presidency. He also intended to make certain that once out of the office he could continue to control the agency by influencing who became its chief. In fact, Calles's old supporter, Francisco Delgado, who headed the agency until 1930, kept Calles informed about opposition to the government. During the provisional presidency of Portes Gil, Calles, in addition to his military duties, remained politically active, creating the Partido Nacional Revolucionario (National Revolutionary Party) during the first week of December 1928. He realized that such a party organization, if strong enough, would contribute to the centralization of power and help institutionalize the Revolution. In March of the next year the new party met in Querétaro to choose a candidate for the presidential election scheduled for 1930. During the proceedings it became

General Joaquín Amaro, Calles's closest military adviser.
Fideicomiso Archivos Plutarco Elías Calles y Fernando Torreblanca. México, DF.

Anti-Calles rebels on the northern frontier, Agua Prieta, 1929.
Arizona Historical Society, Tucson.

clear that Calles supported Pascual Ortiz Rubio to occupy the position. His support was tantamount to election to the office. Although soon in office, Ortiz Rubio was not politically astute enough to survive in the contradictory and difficult political minefield that was then Mexico. He also failed to accept or understand that it was Calles who had placed him in the presidency and who manipulated politics in the country.

In early February Daniel Flores, a little-known twenty-three-year-old, attempted to assassinate Ortiz Rubio. No amount of persuasion could force the attacker to divulge his motives or name accomplices. A witch hunt followed, during which several individuals who had opposed Ortiz Rubio as president were tortured and murdered. Ortiz Rubio recovered from his wounds, but his presidency did not survive. By September 1932, with pressure from important congressmen and army officers that Calles orchestrated, Ortiz Rubio resigned the presidency, leaving Calles to ponder the appointment of the next puppet. After short deliberation, he selected General Abelardo Rodríguez, who was supported in turn by the congress.

Throughout the difficulties the country faced in the late 1920s and early 1930s, Delgado leaked information to Calles. Until 1932, Calles, wielding either his executive power or his political influence, was able to secure the cooperation of several of the secretaries of Gobernación, such as Carlos Riva

Palacio, by sending agents to various regions to investigate the actions of any groups that might threaten their positions. Throughout this period the department continued to undergo changes in leadership. On September 1, 1928, Pablo Meneses became second-in-command of the Departamento Confidencial under Delgado. The new subchief spent little time in the office, choosing instead to meet agents at his home for assignments and reports. He was secretive and sought constantly to insure the clandestine nature of the office and work. Although Delgado continued as the head of the department, he often relied on a subordinate like Meneses to direct the work of agents. During 1929, department operations continued, but fewer records exist for that year. Pastor C. Navarrete, as Adjutant of the Office (Ayudante de la Oficina), apparently assisted in the management of the department, and existing records indicate the office operated smoothly when he was in charge. His former experience as an agent no doubt benefitted him in his dealings with operatives. On May 6, 1930, the department was again reorganized when Riva Palacio became Secretario de Gobernación and appointed Pablo Meneses, who had headed the department briefly during 1928, to return to the agency as chief of the department.

During the five years that Delgado either directly or indirectly operated the Departamento Confidencial, political unrest in the country made all tasks difficult. Delgado closely monitored the activities of the organization, and his assignment as chief of the department had been fortuitous in terms of professionalizing the organization and operating the agency. He had insisted that agents write concise reports, conduct themselves so as not to draw attention to their presence, and promptly report anything they believed might become an immediate problem for the government. He remained dedicated to Calles, and regularly demonstrated this loyalty. He sent agents to monitor labor meetings or report on rumors of antigovernment activities, tried to stifle seditious propaganda, attempted to stop the growing traffic in small arms among rebel groups, and dealt with other serious internal security problems. Under Delgado's guidance the Departamento Confidencial—along with other close confidants Calles appointed at the state and national levels—helped keep Calles in power until 1935, when General Lázaro Cárdenas finally gained control of the country and exiled Calles to the United States.

Delgado's impact on the Departamento Confidencial itself was significant. He was personally acquainted with all of his agents. He insisted that they be professional and well-educated. Many had been medical doctors, lawyers, professors, or businessmen. Occasionally, he employed equally qualified women. The department provided a home telephone for each agent, and Delgado communicated with them frequently and directly. To keep operations clandestine, agents were provided with three different identification cards showing different occupations, and when they sent messages by telegraph, they were ordered to send them in code. Recognizing that his employees had to work irregular hours and frequently travel away from home, Delgado sought to pay them as well as possible. The Government paid the Special Political Information Agents (Agentes Especiales de Información Política) and the Inspectors Second Level (Inspectores de Segunda)[25] a generous salary and gave them a daily expense account sufficient to discharge their duties. Agents did not have railroad passes during this period, but they could use the railroad by showing their police license plates.

During his five years as head of the department, Delgado enjoyed the cooperation of Navarrete, Trinidad García, Coronel Francisco Mayer, and many others. García was in charge of the agency archive from February 8, 1925, until May 15, 1930. Agents José Jesús Gutiérrez, José Merced López, and David Galicia Ortega collaborated with Delgado in conducting police investigations and exposing political threats and clerical plots against the government. Women who worked for Delgado were discreet and competent, and included Ana María Velázquez, who worked in the archive, and Raquel Cárdenas, who took a position in the headquarters office in 1925 and contributed to the work of the department.

By the end of the 1920s, the Departamento Confidencial had demonstrated its usefulness in keeping the Mexican government informed of the social and political conditions in the country. During the next decade the department continued to achieve higher levels of professionalization, and the nature of its assignments also evolved as Mexico began to anticipate a second world war.

CHAPTER 3

EL DEPARTAMENTO CONFIDENCIAL, 1930-1940

During the 1930s, the Departamento Confidencial continued monitoring social and political activities in the country. Until early 1935, the agency chief sent the reports to the office of the Secretario de Gobernación, which then passed the information to Calles. The individuals serving as Secretary of Gobernación during this period were loyal to the Jefe Máximo, as Calles came to be known, or they did not last long in the office. Able to influence who would become president, Calles maintained considerable power in the government, and he wielded this power to remain informed of anything of significance to the government that occurred in the country. He continued allowing local caudillos to control a state as long as they remained loyal to him personally. Although he relied heavily upon party operatives to monitor regional opposition and employed the National Revolutionary Party (PNR) and political patronage to tie regional caudillos to him, he continued to utilize the Departamento Confidencial for gathering information.

Calles remained the most powerful individual in the country until General Lázaro Cárdenas became president in December of 1934. The new president, as soon as possible, appointed his loyal supporters to direct the Departamento Confidencial to assure that he, and not Calles, controlled this valuable internal affairs monitoring agency. Until early 1935, however, the agency undoubtedly helped Calles retain his influence. Calles also assured his domination of Mexican politics through the manipulation of state and local governments—often influencing appointments to local government offices—and through his continuing control of the PNR. From the late 1920s until well into the 1930s, his success with labor groups was due in many respects to his alliance with Luis Morones, who led the Regional Confederation of Mexican Workers (Confederación Regional Obrera Mexicana, or CROM). Calles frequently appointed CROM members to influential administrative positions in local and national government. Morones worked closely with Calles until late in Calles's career, when the former president's political stance began moving considerably to the right. Despite using Morones to accomplish his aims, Calles never trusted him. This distrust was apparent in Calles's frequent deployment of agents of the Departamento Confidencial to monitor meetings of the cromistas.

The Cristero Rebellion against the government had officially ended by 1930, but government retaliations against former cristeros continued until 1932 or later. As long as Calles remained influential in the government, the Departamento Confidencial continued its surveillance of the church and clergy, dispatching agents throughout the country to monitor all manner of ecclesiastical activity. Although Calles had personally selected Emilio Portes Gil, Pascual Ortiz Rubio, and finally General Abelardo Rodríguez to be nominal presidents after Obregón's assassination, he did not trust any of them completely. Consequently, he closely monitored their activities and made certain that the chief of the Departamento Confidencial was loyal only to him. During the early 1930s, Calles's inner circle underwent changes as relations between Morones and Calles began to cool. This change was evident in agency reports reflecting increased monitoring of CROM activities. As Calles moved steadily toward the political right, he became increasingly guarded and defensive. During this period he relied heavily upon the Departamento Confidencial, as well as the party apparatus of the PNR, to shore up his power and gather information on suspected enemies. Messages in the department archives reveal that agency chiefs remained in communication with Calles throughout this period, usually through channels at Gobernación.

During early August 1931, Calles became more concerned about potential opposition from Morones. The Departamento Confidencial dispatched several agents to observe and report upon the meetings of CROM, where, by this time, Morones could be counted on to offer unfavorable comments about opposing labor groups and, indirectly, the government. In one report a Departamento Confidencial agent, who had attended a CROM meeting undercover, informed his chief that he had monitored Morones's meeting, and, in his opinion, the gathering was obviously antigovernment. While Morones did not attack Calles directly, he charged the government in general with being misdirected, involved in intrigue, and abandoning the poor. The agent also reported that Morones rather directly accused some people in the government of being enemies of the Revolution. Calles also faced opposition

President Calles (seated, third from right) with his close associates. Luis Morones is second from left.
Fideicomiso Archivos Plutarco Elías Calles y Fernando Torreblanca. México, DF.

from Communists, who had organized to protest his changes in government policies toward labor, as well as his behind-the-scenes rule of the country. As Calles became increasingly anti-Communist and more conservative, he directed the Departamento Confidencial to send additional agents to monitor Communist activities.

In 1934, Enrique Garza García, chief of the Departamento Confidencial, advised Gobernación that his office remained "indispensable primarily because it was the eyes and ears" of the government. The agency had a large, well-organized archive, and its agents generally cooperated with the army on all security matters. It had investigated antigovernment rebels and had gathered considerable information about the activities of clerics.[1]

During the 1930s, the Departamento Confidencial underwent internal changes to increase efficiency. Various chiefs of the agency lobbied with the government for better pay and an increased budget to create a more effective agency. In early 1930, Pablo Meneses became chief of the agency, earning a salary of twenty-eight pesos per day. He served only until May 1931, but proved an able administrator. He asked that agents receive higher pay, although the request was not granted immediately. He also restructured the department and continued to improve its efficiency. He established specific rules regulating the hours an agent worked. Among his most important changes was a requirement that agents report to the office at 9:00 each morning and sign an attendance book. He required them to sign out for lunch and when they left for the day. Similar rules had existed before Meneses inaugurated new ones, but they had not been enforced. A few agents responded to Meneses's new rules by arriving at the office, signing in, and then leaving, only to return briefly in order to sign out at the end of the day. Meneses quickly put an end to this, although agents complained that to collect information efficiently they needed to be able to move about secretly. They insisted the new rules made it difficult to hide their identities or movements from public purview.

Salary levels impaired recruitment and retention of good agents and staff. Many agents believed they were not paid enough, nor did they receive sufficient travel funds. Gabriel Miranda was subchief at this time and received a salary of sixteen pesos daily, while David Chávez Sierra as First Officer (Oficial Primero) received nine pesos per day. Ana María Velásquez was Fourth Officer (Oficial Cuarto) at six pesos daily. José de la Luz Mena and Rafael Mancera Aldeco, Second Class Inspectors (Inspectores de Segunda), each received fifteen pesos daily, and Luis González Contreras was Inspector Level Seven (Inspector Septima) and received ten pesos daily. Thirteen lower-ranking agents received from six to eight pesos a day, and at least four office staff members were paid only four. (At this time, one peso equaled 0.0777 USD.) In 1931, the agents were further classified as either Political Information Agents (Agentes de Información Política) or Administrative Police Agents (Agentes de Policía Administrativa), the latter working closely with local and federal police. At this point Subchief Lic. Salvador Estrada advised Gobernación that the agents had received the same pay for the last two years. He argued that better pay was needed, insisting that if the Departamento Confidencial wished to recruit people from the more educated classes and expected its agents not to accept bribes, then they must be paid a higher wage.[2]

Meneses next suggested to Gobernación that ten more agents be hired and sent to several states to report specifically on local politics. He also suggested that four agents be hired who would operate entirely undercover. They would report only to the director of the agency and never enter the office. In an early attempt to profile prospective enemies, Meneses also ordered agents to create lists of militant political types and individuals involved in seditious publishing or who advocated a change in government. Gobernación approved only a few of these suggestions.

Despite tepid support from Gobernación, Meneses made several improvements in operations and enlarged the scope of the agency. He sent agents to the United States to monitor the activities of Catholic militants, expatriates of all types, and Communists along the north side of the border. He also for the first time issued identification cards to agents stating that they were journalists or travel agents. He changed the code agents used for reports, making it more difficult for outsiders to translate, but also harder for operatives to use. Agents who were not undercover received license plates for their cars identifying them as employees of Gobernación.

During his tenure as head of the agency, Meneses had two assistant directors, Col. Gabriel Miranda, who served from May 16, 1930, until February of 1931, and Adolfo Granados, whose term lasted from February 1, 1931, until June of that year. These men frequently directed the work of the field agents. Agents who worked for Meneses described Miranda as a nervous individual who did things quickly, though not necessarily carefully. He was not subtle, often charging into a residence or office on the pretext of investigating something only to learn that there was nothing to investigate. Such was the case when, in the spring of 1931, upon hearing rumors of armed, angry workers, he barged into the headquarters of the Workers' Party (Partido del Obrero y Campesino Mexicano) in Mexico City only to learn the rumors were groundless. On several occasions, his indiscretions were described in the next day's newspapers, raising concern and causing embarrassment for high-ranking government officials. Granados got along better with agents and with Meneses than Miranda did, following and relaying Meneses's orders accurately to the agents. Still, Granados found working with the director to be a challenge. Meneses was competent but excitable, difficult, and unpredictable, none of which were good characteristics for the head of a clandestine organization.[3]

Internal disagreements in the Departamento Confidencial sometimes led agents and the chief to neglect their work. Meneses was evidently unhappy with his assignment, especially when he had to resolve serious personnel conflicts within the agency. He was frequently absent, leaving the administration of the agency to his second-in-command. Shortly before Miranda filled the position, in May 1930, Pastor C. Navarrete resigned his post as subchief of the agency, complaining that Meneses was a thief, a murderer, and a supporter of prostitution and gambling in Mexico City. He charged that Meneses's criminal involvement brought him a great deal of money in the form of payoffs for the lax handling of situations that clearly merited thorough investigation. Navarrete publicly accused Meneses and agent Valente Quintana of committing serious transgressions against individuals and violating Mexican laws.[4] He submitted no proof to support these charges, and there was apparently no evidence to substantiate the claims.

Meneses, evidently tired of being accused of illegal activities, resigned his position. On May 11, 1931, Colonel Adalberto Torres Estrada became chief of the Departamento Confidencial, serving until September 6, 1932. Torres Estrada had a close relationship with President Abelardo Rodríguez, and after his appointment as agency chief, he devoted considerable time to working on special projects for the president. When Torres Estrada was away from the office on these assignments, he delegated his authority to his assistant director, Major Francisco Beas Mendoza, a graduate of the Mexican Military College (Colegio Militar). Torres Estrada required that Beas Mendoza inform him each week of departmental activities, and he relayed this information directly to Rodríguez as well as Calles.

Under Beas Mendoza's leadership, the agency continued to improve its operation. He divided the agents into five groups to carry out special assignments. The first group of three agents dealt with police affairs, local political delegations, and other local matters. The second, also comprised of three agents, scrutinized the activities of the Secretary of War and other public officials, monitored local military activities, examined the operations of the Secretary of the Treasury, and spied on railroad workers' organizations. The third, also three agents, followed Communist, agrarian, and labor actions; reported on the activities of the Knights of Columbus; and kept an eye on shows in theaters, movies, bars, and cabarets. The fourth group also had three agents who were assigned to watch all political groups, gather daily press information, and monitor public transportation. The fifth, with four agents, monitored the Chamber of Deputies and the Senate, and reported on the activities of the National Revolutionary Party, the Secretary of Communications, including telegraph and mail, and foreigners in the country. Upon completion of an assignment, each agent wrote a daily report and sent it to the chief of the department, who then forwarded it to Gobernación. Beas Mendoza served only fifty-six days in his role as chief of the agency, but through his specific requirements for agents, he improved its efficiency.

Early in July, Sálvador Estrada Martínez became chief of the Departamento Confidencial. One unidentified agent remarked that the new chief was not personally impressive and looked like a decrepit old man as he walked. He did not function in his position in that manner, however. He received his appointment as a reward for his loyalty to the president, but he proved an adequate administrator. He named his close friend Eduardo Moguel, a man with a reputation for hard work, to a supervisory position. Moguel was ambitious and capable and did most of the work of running the office. In the meantime Estrada Martínez lobbied for more funds to be allotted to the department, asking that funding be set at $85,410 pesos for the next fiscal year, almost doubling the previous year's rate. He planned to keep sixteen agents employed at all times, covering such issues as federal criminals, the expulsion of pernicious foreigners from the country, and the investigation of political and religious matters. These agents would also be available twenty-four hours a day for assignment. He intended to employ only agents well-versed in the laws of the country and, like Meneses, insisted they be paid well enough to discourage corruption. He believed the chief and assistant chief must also receive decent wages.[5] Shortly after Estrada Martínez formally offered these suggestions, agents began studying the English language as well as US and Mexican laws. The agents were also armed: a departmental inventory at the time listed twenty-nine pistols and a significant quantity of ammunition.

By mid 1932 changes were underway in agency protocol as the agency continued to monitor general political matters, all activities of the Catholic Church, the actions of members of the national Chamber of Deputies, the presidential residence, the PNR, the National Palace, theaters and entertainment centers, and sometimes various foreign political delegations.[6] Once finished with an assignment, agents devoted considerable time to writing detailed notes for the director of the agency. Office staff took these and then wrote abstracts of the activities and reports, identifying the agent only by number. These reports often included information about what governors in the various states were saying or doing, what high-ranking army officers said or did, and what occurred in any public demonstrations against the local or national government. Agents continued to report to Calles, who was keeping tabs on such individuals as General Lázaro Cárdenas, who was extremely powerful in his home state of Michoacán.[7]

Despite the changes in operation made by the various directors, individuals within and outside the government criticized the Departamento Confidencial throughout the early 1930s, charging that it was inefficient, that various chiefs had sought to profit from their position, and that the organization was not professionally administered. There was an element of truth to the charges. In 1933, Francisco M. Delgado, who had directed the agency from 1925 to 1930, responded to criticism of the agency in a note to Calles. In 1930, Delgado had left the agency to accept another government position, where he had been very satisfied; however, he told Calles that he was aware of how far the Departamento Confidencial had "deteriorated" since his departure. He was willing to return to his position as agency head, if Calles so desired. Delgado said he required no pay, as he felt an obligation to serve his country and especially Calles. He recognized that many people had taken advantage of Mexico's relative individual freedoms to conspire against the government. Finally, Delgado claimed that he built a successful career in government and wished to remain in Mexico City so his children could get a good education.

The fact that Delgado wrote Calles, who was not officially in power, indicates that he and other informed Mexicans recognized the former president's continuing influence. During this period, others shared Delgado's concern that the Departamento Confidencial was no longer operating efficiently and suggested that many of its functions be transferred to a new Mexican Secret Service. Problems within the agency were related in many respects to politics, as agency chiefs and investigators often received their appointments as political favors. Too often, agents were much more dedicated to receiving a government salary than they were to their work.[8] In January 1934, Dr. Enrique Durand of Tehuantepec, Oaxaca, wrote President Rodríguez that Mexico should create a new Secret Service of Investigation and Espionage (Servicio Secreto de Investigación y Espionaje) modeled upon the secret agencies the Germans operated during World War I. Durand believed the Departamento Confidencial was unable to discharge its duties adequately because it failed to maintain extreme secrecy.[9] Some of the functions he suggested for this new service were already performed by various government agencies, but he believed that a truly secret service did not yet exist.

In response to criticism of the Departamento Confidencial, General Joaquín de la Peña, who had become director in January 1934, inaugurated new rules for the operation of the agency. He established a hierarchy within the organization in which he specified that agents were to report to the chief or subchief only. The chain of command was not to be violated for any reason. He also required each agent to keep careful records of daily activities and expenditures. He divided the investigative division of the agency into two agent classes called Inspectors of Investigation and Agents of Investigation (Inspectores de Investigación and Agentes de Investigación), neither of which could admit to being part of the department. Agents had to be discreet, honest, honorable, disciplined, diligent, decent, and wise. They had to be of conspicuously good conduct and clearly understand their responsibilities. When agents were operating within the Federal District, they were required to report daily by telephone at certain hours and be at their residences at 10:00 and 16:00 to receive orders. Written reports were to be concise, simple, precise, and impartial, and agents were expected to use correct Spanish in written reports and while conducting investigations. Other requirements defined appropriate office behavior, established when reports were due, and set myriad other requirements, including continuing education about the history, traditions, and laws of the country. This was a serious attempt to eliminate some of the problems within the agency and to make it more productive.[10] Because of these and earlier measures taken to professionalize the agency, at times the Departamento Confidencial actually conducted its business fairly efficiently, though there remained room for improvement.

By the early 1930s, Calles was becoming almost daily more sensitive to criticism and threats from any sector of society. Concerned about growing resistance, the ex-president apparently asked the Departamento Confidencial to intensify its investigation of all groups that opposed his influence in government. He faced considerable opposition from the Communists and other leftists who had organized to protest government changes in policies toward labor. In addition to disliking his ever-more conservative political position, these groups also resented his continuing influence in the government. During the first week of August 1931, an agent assigned to observe Communist activities in Mexico City reported that the local Communist weekly *El Machete* had urged workers to rise up against the government and take their protests to the streets. This urging prompted two hundred Communists to march through the central downtown area to the Chamber of Deputies. The mob entered the Chamber building and delivered a strong anti-Calles petition, denouncing Calles and his followers as liars and demagogues. Almost immediately, armed government troops and police confronted the group and forced them out of the building, where they faced another group of mounted and armed police who sent the protesters packing.

In 1934, as the presidential election of that year approached, more confrontations and violence between police, government troops, and political factions occurred throughout the country. Agents of the Departamento Confidencial closely monitored these outbreaks. At one point an agent traveled to Apizaco, Tlaxcala, to investigate the murder of Edmundo Rangel, who had become involved in local political violence. According to the agent's report, Rangel had supported Madero and, later, Carranza. Callistas in the state believed he was strongly anti-Calles, a risky stance. Moreover, from what the agent could gather, Rangel had few scruples and an inflated opinion of himself. Some local citizens described him as "irascible, intolerant, impulsive, constantly blasphemous, and disposed to drinking too much." He was contentious, demonstrated animosity towards authority, and "most important, opposed Governor Bonillas."[11] Once the agent probed a bit deeper, he learned that the governor had tried to coerce Rangel's cooperation, but Rangel, an influential attorney, refused to accept the local power structure and was positioning himself to replace Bonillas as governor, or at least to acquire a share of local power in the state. The agent's report implied that Rangel's opposition to the governor led directly to his murder.

Later that year, another agent traveled to Michoacán to report on local elections. He noted conflict between agraristas (agrarian workers) and local authorities during the late hours of voting. Alerted by his report, the government sent federal troops to the city, where they arrived just as shooting began. A few agraristas were wounded in the exchange of gunfire.

Around this time the Departamento Confidencial sent two agents to Dolores Hidalgo, Guanajuato, to investigate the murders of two local politicians, one of whom had led campesinos in confrontations with state and local authorities. The agents' sources informed them that a few days before the murders, a federal congressional deputy, José Martínez Vértiz, was seen in local bars offering four hundred pesos to anyone who would carry out the murders. The situation became more suspicious when local police arrived two hours after the killings, were given descriptions of the killers and informed of their whereabouts, yet chose not to pursue them. According to the agents' report, the local police captain insisted the two men described by witnesses were not the guilty parties. Instead, police arrested an old man, Eleutario González, who had observed the murders and given authorities a good description of the shooter. González spent four days in jail until his memory of the event conveniently faded, and he was released. The agents said rumors were circulating that the governor of the state had ordered the murders.[12] Violence of this nature was common during the period, and agents of the Departamento Confidencial frequently reported such incidents to the chief of the agency.

By now, Calles was aware that his power in the country was waning, and he tried to protect his influence by supporting someone for the presidency he thought he could control. Younger politicians and army officers were less inclined to fear him, and therefore less likely to do his bidding. He believed there was at least a chance of finding an adequate puppet in General Lázaro Cárdenas. Unfortunately for Calles, he soon found he was mistaken.

Cárdenas rose to a position of prominence as a military officer during the Mexican Revolution, proving himself an able soldier and politician. By 1920, as a leading brigadier general, he had positioned himself to wield considerable influence in his home state of Michoacán. Between 1928 and 1932, while remaining an army general, he served as governor of this state. He supported Obregón, Calles, and Abelardo Rodríguez during the 1920s and early 1930s, although he was significantly more reform-minded and leftist in his political ideology. During 1933 and 1934, he did not at first overtly seek the Mexican presidency, but made himself a viable candidate by dealing carefully with Calles so as not to alienate him. His political career was further bolstered when President Rodríguez appointed him Minister of War, placing Cárdenas in the national government and positioning him to grow in power and importance.

Since 1928 and Obregón's assassination, Calles had manipulated the appointment of two interim presidents and the election of a third. It was clear that he wished to see a candidate he could continue to control as the next PNR nominee, and thus the next president. Through the first part of 1933 Cárdenas had resisted declaring himself a candidate for the presidency, but in May of that year he resigned his post as War Minister to make himself available for the office. Calles initially supported Cárdenas for the presidency, but as 1933 progressed and Cárdenas appealed to labor and agrarian interests for support, Calles must have questioned whether he would be able to control him once in office. Calles suffered ill health during the summer of 1933, and partly for this reason left Mexico City for Ensenada, Baja California, where, he declared, he could rest and recover. He also realized that it might be wise to stay out of the capital during this particularly contentious period of selecting the next president.

By January of 1934, Cárdenas had garnered sufficient public support to be nominated as the PNR candidate, and he finally accepted the formal nomination that spring. Calles did not oppose him, still hoping to be able to influence him once in office. Calles also counted on many callista caudillos and military officers to support him in any struggle with Cárdenas. Although Cárdenas faced opposition from the candidates of other political groups, on July 1, 1934, he won an overwhelming victory.

On December 1, 1934, Cárdenas assumed the presidency, and—well aware of Calles's continued political meddling—slowly but systematically removed loyal callistas from positions of power in the government, the army, and the Departamento Confidencial.[13] Cárdenas was aware that the method Calles (and other previous presidents) had used to control the country was to allow state strongmen, usually governors who had ascended to the rank of general during the Revolution, to retain their influence as long as they remained loyal to him personally as well as to the government and the PNR.

Cárdenas knew that in order to change the political system, he either had to have the cooperation of these power brokers, or he had to separate them from their power bases.

Within a few months after assuming office, Cárdenas set about to professionalize the army. He retired the old callista army officers who had risen to high rank during the disorganized fighting of the Revolution, and granted them pensions. He then replaced them with younger men he believed he could trust. He transferred generals remaining on active duty out of their home states and placed them in commands across the country, in order to break the grip these individuals had on local areas and thus weaken their power bases. He insisted upon curriculum changes at the Colegio Militar with the aim of improving military education. He also provided better weapons and encouraged further measures to modernize the military and foster their loyalty to the new political system he was creating. He hoped this would eventually lead to nonpolitical, high-ranking army officers taking command of the army. All of the changes Cárdenas called for moved Mexico toward a more institutionalized political system controlled from the nation's capital.

No longer in control of the presidency, Calles recognized Cárdenas's attempts to consolidate his power and began to criticize the new president. The more strident and aggressive Calles became in his opposition, the more determined Cárdenas was to eliminate his influence both in the national regime and in the regional governments. In 1935, once in complete control of the Departamento Confidencial, Cárdenas turned the tables on the expresident and his cohorts in Mexico City and the various states, ordering the agency to monitor their every move. The director of the department sent several agents to observe Calles wherever he traveled, and for a period they remained outside the Calles home in Mexico City day and night. On one occasion, an agent reported that a group of men had met with Calles with the aim of founding a periodical to be called *Independientes*, which was designed to attack the Cárdenas government. Additionally, the agent learned that Calles supporters, including several workers' groups, were trying to organize a labor strike for the end of April that would paralyze the country.[14]

In May of 1935, the Departamento Confidencial dispatched agent Ignacio H. Santana to Bermejillo, Durango, to report on a rumored callista uprising. In Bermejillo, callista-inspired opposition had developed against

Cárdenas's gubernatorial candidate and other local municipal authorities who favored the president. In fact, callista governors controlled more than thirty Mexican states, and Cárdenas viewed this as a significant threat. He sought to place his supporters in leadership positions in every state, so that local caudillos would lose the power to control their constituents through political patronage. Eventually, Cárdenas won this battle for local control, but not without some violence and some clever political maneuvering. There is little doubt that using the Departamento Confidencial to monitor these situations helped Cárdenas protect his regime and place his faithful in important political positions.[15]

Early in 1936, Cárdenas decided that Calles's presence in Mexico was too deleterious to his presidency and the reforms and progress that he wished for the country. The solution to this problem, he believed, was to exile Calles and several of his most faithful cronies. On April 10, 1936, Cárdenas dispatched high-ranking army officers and troops to escort Calles and his entourage to the airport, where they were loaded aboard an aircraft bound for the United States. Cárdenas warned them in the strongest terms not to return. Calles and close associates ultimately settled in California, where they remained until the end of the Cárdenas sexenio (six-year term as President), fearing for their lives. None of these exiles returned while Cárdenas was in power.

By exiling Calles and reorganizing the army, Cárdenas effectually served notice that he alone would lead the government and determine Mexico's internal and external policies. It soon became apparent to all political sectors that he intended to move the government to the left, supporting policies that would provide greater opportunities for those in the agrarian and labor sectors who had not enjoyed the benefits of a modernizing Mexico. Cárdenas sincerely wanted to help the country's poor and dispossessed by improving the living conditions of all Mexicans who lived in abject poverty. He was particularly concerned about those peasants suffering in isolated, primarily indigenous populations. To address the country's economic disparities, the president created a considerable number of agricultural communities (ejidos), wherein hundreds of families worked common lands while practicing subsistence agriculture on small plots allotted to individual families. He dedicated his government to improving education, health, sanitary conditions, and quality of life for these individuals. While Cárdenas's aim in these programs was to help the lowest classes, he was simultaneously shifting the campesinos' loyalties from the local caudillos to the national government. Henceforth, agrarian and labor interests were dealt with on a national level.

Cárdenas's leftist politics also shaped government policy toward foreign oil interests. By the time he exiled Calles to California, Cárdenas had notified foreign businesses that they must cooperate with the government in respect to labor and national resources in Mexico or face potential nationalization of their assets. Although concerned about other foreign investment, Cárdenas was particularly concerned about the petroleum industry. When foreign-owned petroleum companies balked at his requests to renegotiate union contracts, he warned the companies that not cooperating would lead to government retaliation. Eventually Cárdenas grew weary of the recalcitrance of the companies, and on March 18, 1938, in order to protect workers and the sovereignty of Mexico, he nationalized all foreign oil holdings in the country. Thereafter, his administration changed the laws under which foreign companies operated in Mexico. Cárdenas believed that Mexicans should control all natural resources and were entitled to reap greater profits from the output of corporations operating on Mexican soil. Conservative Mexican and foreign business interests opposed this political shift to the left, but they could do nothing to forestall it. Again in this instance, Cárdenas was a clear winner politically, a result he surely expected. Nationalizing the oil companies was extremely popular among the Mexican people, and this gained him political support for carrying out yet more of his policies.

Despite heated opposition to Cárdenas from conservatives in Mexico and corporate leaders in the United States, no armed revolt erupted. By the late 1930s, the United States, facing an increasing threat from Nazi Germany and Imperial Japan, was reluctant to alienate Mexico. President Franklin D. Roosevelt, as part of his Good Neighbor Policy of the early 1930s, continuously sought to maintain good relations with Mexico and other Latin American countries. Until Cárdenas left office in 1940, however, he continued to face strong opposition from powerful, conservative business elites in all sections of Mexico.

Cárdenas was particularly wary of business and industrial conservatives in Nuevo León and other northern states who opposed government intervention in their affairs. These leaders did not subscribe to government's managing the economic life of the country when it interfered with their business-es or usurped their political and military power. Dedicated to laissez-faire economic policies, they had established and financed the Confederación Pa-tronal de la República Mexicana (COPARMEX), an organization they used to promote their political beliefs. When the Cárdenas government tried to organize workers in a factory in Monterrey, violence erupted. The north-ern conservatives refused to cave in to the Cárdenas policies, and in 1940 they would initially support conservative General Juan Andreu Almazán for president.[16]

While Cárdenas, like his predecessors, continued to use the Departa-mento Confidencial as one method of gathering political and social infor-mation and maintaining control of the country, he was also aware of the importance of the government political party, the PNR. Soon after he na-tionalized the petroleum industry, Cárdenas reorganized the government's party and changed its name to the Partido Revolucionario Mexicano (PRM). In the PRM he created a new structural organization that incorporated mul-tiple groups, including the military and popular sectors. Combined with his efforts to replace old revolutionary generals with younger professional soldiers, Cárdenas's incorporation of the army into the PRM contributed to ending the army's frequent intervention in politics and ultimately led to its removal from the political arena. Now the army would work through the party to protect its position in the country. While Calles had created the first national party in the PNR, Cárdenas moved to reorganize the Revolution-ary party in a way that would continue to weaken the power of the regional caudillos.

By late 1935, Cárdenas took firm control of all aspects of government, including the Departamento Confidencial. Agents loyal to Calles had been purged, and their replacements knew they now served the new president. In 1936, Jesús A. Tostado, unquestionably loyal to Cárdenas, became chief of the agency. In addition to duties monitoring Calles and the various political sectors, his agents were dedicated to uncovering any antigovernment plots or activities that might destabilize the country. Agents ranged throughout the country investigating local politicians and labor organizations and in-forming Cárdenas of potential threats.

During 1936, agent Alfredo León traveled to Acapulco to monitor local elections. Cárdenas wished to see one of his adherents win the governor-ship, and he hoped to influence who won. The agent's reports indicated that the local situation was unremarkable and generally peaceful. He had heard, however, that one of the candidates held pro-Communist beliefs. He did not specifically name this individual, possibly because he knew he was reporting rumor. The agent suggested that this candidate had considerable support in the area and if he lost the election, his supporters would likely rebel against the established political order, perhaps taking up arms.[17] Such rebellions, of course, were something Cárdenas wanted to thwart wherever possible.

Another agent, Herminio Lugo, traveled to Cuautitlán in the state of Mexico to investigate the bombing of a Masonic lodge. He claimed he could not determine who was guilty of this attack, but he believed they were fanat-ics involved "with the callista elements" who wished to create problems. In any event, he assured the agency, the perpetrators were antigovernment.[18] This report was typical of those written by agents who observed or heard about antigovernment activities. It was as if the agent, unable to uncover real evidence, felt compelled to place blame on Calles supporters in order to justify his efforts and expenditures.

Clearly, Cárdenas employed the Departamento Confidencial in much the same manner that Calles had. Like Calles, Cárdenas used the agency to monitor his enemies and undermine threats to his rule, but he also used it to collect general information about politics and society that would help him further institutionalize the political system. Some supporters of the Cárdenas government, however, did not believe the agency was sufficient for monitoring threats to the leadership of the country, and they believed that a well-organized secret service should be established to replace the agency. Late in 1937, Army Captain Salvador Amezcua F. wrote to Cárdenas that such a service could monitor "moment by moment" everything that hap-pened in the country. He suggested the creation of three divisions, including a Secret Service (Dirección del Servicio Secreto, or DSS), a Special Agents Group (Grupo de Agentes Especiales, or GAE), and Information Agents (Agentes de Información, or AI). The DSS would operate undercover and report only to the president. Publicly, to maintain secrecy, it would be called the Department of Publicity and Propaganda (Departamento de Publicidad y Propaganda) [19] Apparently, Cárdenas did not take Amezcua's suggestion to heart. Nonetheless, he continued to use the PRM and the Departamento Confidencial to achieve similar ends.

During the Cárdenas presidency, agents of the Departamento Confidencial became more efficient as they underwent increasingly specialized training. They conformed to stricter requirements for conduct and received a more thorough education in Mexican history and politics. The focus of agent reports became broader and frequently more analytical. For example, during 1936, agent Ignacio H. Santana traveled to Durango, Guanajuato, among other states, to investigate the general social and political conditions there. He frequently submitted long reports containing his analyses. On one occasion, he submitted a typed, single-spaced, highly detailed five-page report. He divided his information into sections, including criminal information, where he reported rumors of dynamite bombs ready to be planted in government offices; political information, which contained his commentary about a local police inspector's competence and loyalty; and social information, in which he discussed his visits to schools to follow accusations of Cristero influence on students. In this report, Santana listed all the candidates for local office, analyzed their political positions vis-à-vis national issues, and discussed the political biases of local authorities in respect to local and national candidates. He also described the political attitude of the local army commander, appraised his potential for interfering in the electoral process, and disclosed whether or not local officials were observing electoral laws.[20]

Similar information filtered through the agency to Cárdenas on a regular basis. The intelligence provided by agent L. Lozano García in March 1936, from Acámbaro, Guanajuato, was typical of agency reporting during the Cárdenas era. Lozano García relayed what he had discovered in his investigation and speculated on the likelihood of a major problem developing in the region. He uncovered a plot to plant a bomb near a federal school building, where President Cárdenas planned to hold a town meeting in the near future. This information prompted local authorities to search the premises carefully, but they found nothing, although in fact someone *had* placed a box of dynamite in the building. On February 28, at 3:00 a.m., the building exploded. Cárdenas was not near the building, nor was anyone else, but since dynamite was highly unstable, the explosion may have been triggered accidentally. The agent reported to his superiors that the perpetrators were either clerics, callistas, or perhaps partisans of the present governor, one Cárdenas wanted to replace. Agent Lozano García did not believe the local police inspector was involved in any of this. He claimed that "despite the fact that the inspector was just a campesino, and had no previous police experience, he worked hard and was a strong supporter of Cárdenas." The agent concluded his report by providing general political and social information about the region.[21]

Three months later, Lozano García was investigating rumors of political strife in Tampico, Tamaulipas, when he again offered his analysis of a local situation. He provided his office with varying impressions and offered some commentary about local public opinion, and he suggested explanations for the "different aspects of the political and social life in the state." He explained that the state harbored an active leftist political front organization (Frente Popular de Izquierda), which was promoting a candidate for governor that Cárdenas did not support. Lozano García said that workers' organizations were agitated, and that these groups had organized a demonstration in Ciudad Madero in favor of the opposing gubernatorial candidate. The agent added that he'd heard "angry denouncements against the local government in Tamaulipas." Once again, his report included additional information about the region's political and social conditions.[22]

During this era there were many local squabbles over who would control a state. These confrontations frequently resulted in politically motivated assassinations. The Departamento Confidencial regularly sent agents to investigate these killings. For example, in June 1936, agent Jesús García Ramírez was dispatched to Tepic, Nayarit, to investigate the murder of a twenty-six-year-old individual named Jesús López, who had an alleged criminal record. López had opposed the local state governor, and local authorities had jailed him for unspecified crimes. He was soon released with no charges. He became a delegate to the regional meeting of the Mexican Peasants' Confederation (Confederación Campesina Mexicana). A few days after this appointment, two men followed him to his home, where they shot and killed him in front of his mother. The agent discovered that the two killers were brothers. In García Ramírez's opinion, the killings were politically motivated. The mother told the agent that two power brokers in local politics had ordered her son's murder because of a squabble within the local party organization. García Ramírez found that those responsible for his murder had been arrested briefly, then mysteriously released with no charges. Later, these perpetrators, who were "pistoleros del gobernador," killed the president and the secretary of the local agrarian committee. People traveling the road outside town discovered the two agrarian leaders hanging from a tree. Local authorities cut the men down, hauled off the bodies, and apparently forgot about the incident. The agent reported that seven or eight individuals in all had died at the hands of thugs working for the governor.[23]

Agents of the Departamento Confidencial conducted investigations in every state of the republic, and their reports included local matters as well as national affairs. That same year (1936), agency chief Tostado sent Eliseo Castro Reina to Puebla to report on a demonstration against the local governor and military commander, General Maximino Avila Camacho, the brother of future president Manuel Avila Camacho (1940–1946). Twelve thousand workers of the Regional Workers' and Peasants' Front (Frente Regional de Obreros y Campesinos, or FROC) had held a noisy demonstration in front of the governor's palace in Puebla. This uprising was instigated by the murder of some of the workers, probably at the order of Maximino. The demonstrators demanded that the general be removed from power. Castro Reina reported that an angry and aggressive crowd gathered shouting, "Viva Cárdenas," and proclaiming, "Muera Portes Gil, Muera Avila Camacho." The workers were armed and apparently eager to start shooting. One of them rose to address the agitated crowd. He acknowledged that Maximino was protected by his brother, the powerful General Manuel Avila Camacho, in the national government, but he declared that this should not mitigate Maximino's punishment. The local workers believed that the church also protected Maximino because his mother was a good Catholic. They charged that Maximino had, on many occasions, ordered the killing of leaders of workers' groups in Puebla. Specifically, they charged that in 1934 he had ordered his troops to machine-gun several strikers. In fact, Maximino was known widely for his corruption and brutality, and he frequently responded violently toward the campesinos or others who dared oppose him. While the Cárdenas government had long known of Maximino's tactics, it apparently chose to ignore his transgressions. Evidently Cárdenas felt he needed the support of both brothers.

A typical agent assignment in Puebla can be found in a note from Cipriano Arriola, Chief of the Departamento Confidencial, directing one of his operatives to look into the disappearance of two men. María Cepeda de Montaño and Julia Ramírez Martínez, both of whom lived in San Gabriel Chilac, Puebla, had written to the agency asking that an investigation be launched to discover what had happened to their husbands. The agent learned that local police had jailed the two men in Tehuacán, Puebla, for rather murky reasons, and then released them. When the two men exited the jail, a car stopped and several men forced them into the vehicle. This was the last time they were ever seen.

Such activity was common in the state during Maximino's rule.[24] The campesinos in Puebla knew he had ordered many murders, but they were powerless to stop his horrific violence, and while Cárdenas turned a blind eye, hired thugs continued to punish campesino leaders for any signs of opposition. Surprisingly, the workers did not blame Cárdenas for the murderous behavior of Maximino. The lower classes apparently had no idea how the political system worked. In fact, agents of the Departamento Confidencial heard locals excuse their president by saying that if only Cárdenas were not ill, he would help them.[25] Cárdenas, need it be said, was not ill, but he clearly wanted to maintain control of Puebla, and Maximino was a means to that end.

Nor was Maximino's brutality an isolated case. Local strongmen in all parts of the country regularly used violence to control opposition. Agent Castro Reina worked tirelessly in many other sections of the country, reporting to his superiors the violence he heard about or witnessed firsthand during his investigations. Although the information was most likely passed up the line to the Cárdenas administration, nothing was done to mitigate the widespread use of violence as a means of controlling the populace.

While he was in San Lorenzo Cacaotepec, Oaxaca, Castro Reina learned that local police often arrested campesinos illegally. Oaxacan campesinos told the agent that the local governor had been elected fraudulently, that he was intolerant of anyone who opposed him and brutal in his reprisals. It was even rumored that the governor occasionally hired hit men to assassinate those who were uncooperative.[26] A typical scenario in the region began with a demonstration that led to a physical confrontation, at which point government troops or police would start shooting. Castro Reina reported that the local governor hardly cared who was killed in any given melee.

Another documented instance of government-sponsored retaliation occurred in the northern reaches of the country. In Durango, Castro Reina investigated local elections and learned that the governor had jailed opposition leader José Campos for distributing antigovernment propaganda that contained a picture of his opponent. Although this activity was not illegal, the governor refused to tolerate this type of campaigning.[27]

The disappearance, abduction, and murder of campesinos and workers who spoke out against the local or national government persisted throughout Cárdenas's presidency. Cárdenas was no doubt aware of at least some of these instances, but he chose to remain idle as long as the governor or military commander in the region, who were often one and the same, supported him and the agenda of the PRM. Although Cárdenas did not frequently face serious opposition to his rule, discontent with his policies existed.

Conservative business elites, particularly in Nuevo León, and to some extent in other states, frequently took exception to the Cárdenas effort to organize workers in local industries under the Mexican Workers' Confederation, or CTM (Confederación de Trabajadores de México), which was designed as a counterpoise to the CROM. Cárdenas intended for this new labor sector to support his political agenda, which included, among other things, the expropriation of the assets of several multinational companies. Attempts to nationalize these industries led to labor unrest and strikes throughout the country, however. In the middle of 1936, continuing labor strife in the frontier led to considerable violence, prompting Cárdenas to set aside his immediate work schedule and travel to Monterrey to seek a settlement. On this trip, Cárdenas hoped to establish the CTM among the industries in the region. Despite his efforts, however, the region's labor problems remained unresolved, and after he nationalized petroleum assets—a popular move among most of his constituents—Cárdenas began a slow retreat from leftist policies.[28]

Under the Cárdenas regime, the most serious opposition to the national government occurred as a consequence of the rebellion of General Saturnino Cedillo. A Revolutionary era leader, Cedillo served as governor of San Luis Potosí from 1927 to 1931, as Secretary of Agriculture under President Pascual Ortiz Rubio in 1931, and in the same position for Cárdenas during 1936 and 1937.[29] Cedillo had risen to prominence during the rebellion against President Venustiano Carranza between 1917 and 1920, when he raised an army of agrarian peasants (agraristas) to support Obregón, de la Huerta, Calles, and others in the overthrow of the Carranza regime. After Carranza's demise, Cedillo confiscated large haciendas in his home state and redistributed land in individual parcels to the agraristas. This group recognized that they owed their land and privileges to Cedillo, and they were willing to take up arms on his behalf. For all intents and purposes, then, Cedillo had a private army. In 1920, during his interim presidency, de la Huerta officially recognized Cedillo's military rank as a reward for his assistance against Carranza, placing him and his officers on the government payroll and naming him a district military commander in San Luis Potosí. With such an armed power base, Cedillo would be a threat to any president who wished to centralize authority in Mexico City. Calles had allowed him to retain his army and his influence as long as he brought his forces to the government's aid when it put down rebellions—and remained loyal to Calles personally.

In 1933 and 1934, Cedillo supported Cárdenas for the presidency, holding meetings in San Luis Potosí to unify support for the candidate.[30] Cedillo, like Calles, assumed that Cárdenas would continue on the path established by his predecessors, allowing state caudillos to control their regions and retain their private armies as they had since the Mexican Revolution. Cárdenas, however, intended to end the independence of regional caudillos and provide more land to agrarian peasants. Cárdenas anticipated that Cedillo would oppose his changes, once he realized how they would affect him, and from the outset Cárdenas made certain that an undercover agent of the Departamento Confidential monitored all Cedillo's activities. Even though Cedillo was supporting Cárdenas's candidacy during the presidential campaign, early reports illuminate how intently the agency would follow Cedillo's actions. An agent reported that one meeting at Cedillo's house had included representatives from the Agrarian Leagues (Ligas Agrarias) in the state, and that Cedillo wanted to unify all public sectors in support of Cárdenas for president. The agent seemed to be warning the government when he reported that Cedillo was quite popular in Querétaro, adding that a street had recently been named after him. Cedillo and other pro-Cárdenas supporters held additional meetings, but it was clear from the first that they were more conservative than the candidate. Some of the conservatives in the state were outwardly hostile to Cárdenas.[31]

Once Cárdenas was in office, Cedillo finally realized that the new president aimed to restructure the political system and redistribute lands to agraristas in the form of cooperative ejidos rather than in parcels to individuals, and he concluded that the changes would not be to his benefit. Cedillo and his followers also opposed Cárdenas's effort to bring the local peasantry under the umbrella of the PNR, which would remove them from any organization with strong local ties.

Cárdenas was aware that his leftist programs would meet with resistance, but he was determined not to allow anything or anyone to interfere with his efforts to create a corporate state with a centralized government. He did, however, recognize Cedillo's popularity. Cedillo enjoyed support among the agrarian classes in San Luis Potosí, and from members of the Confederación de la Clase Media (CCM), who like Cedillo, wanted individual ejidos. Cedillo also enjoyed the support of many wealthy Mexican conservatives, the Catholic Church, and United States businessmen with investments south of the international border. The Gold Shirts (Camisas Doradas) supported him with propaganda. Named for the color of their attire, the Doradas were a profascist organization with possible ties to the conservative Sinarquista movement. In some sections of the country, such as San Luis Potosí and Nuevo León, this organization enjoyed appreciable support. For the most part, the leaders of this group were unwilling to take up arms against the Cárdenas government. When in 1935 they were involved in armed fighting, it was against Communists, and they focused their struggle in the Federal District.

Many locally influential leaders agreed with Cedillo and promised to stand against Cárdenas with him, but Cedillo was unwilling to revolt openly against a president who, if government propaganda could be trusted, enjoyed broad popularity.

In June of 1935, Cárdenas made a strategic move when he appointed Cedillo secretary of agriculture. The appointment was designed to lure Cedillo from his local power base and place him in the Federal District. Cedillo foolishly agreed, believing that being in the president's cabinet would strengthen his position in San Luis Potosí. But getting Cedillo out of his home state would free Cárdenas to remove from local offices anyone in San Luis Potosí who did not support the Cárdenas presidency—thus cutting Cedillo's power base out from under him.

By early 1937, Cedillo learned from his supporters in his home state that the president was removing Cedillo supporters from state and federal positions. He realized that in order to protect his interests, he must return at least temporarily to his home state. His visit made it apparent that it was too late for him to do anything to protect himself, for by this time Cárdenas had utilized workers' organizations, strikes, and the strengthened CTM to dismantle Cedillo's base of power. Cárdenas also had redistributed more agricultural lands, thus obligating recipients to the central government. Henceforth, they would depend on the national government for patronage, and not Cedillo.

Cárdenas's removal of cedillistas from positions of influence had critically weakened Cedillo's power. On June 20, 1937, elections of federal deputies in San Luis Potosí provided the setting for an outbreak of violence. Cedillo wanted his cronies elected, but Cárdenas would not tolerate this. Rebellious cedillistas accused the cardenistas in the state of election irregularities and attacked national government officials, wounding at least one and setting the stage for a much larger confrontation between the president and Cedillo, and ultimately between armed cedillistas and the federal army. Cárdenas did not retreat from this violence, ordering federal troops to take whatever measures necessary to maintain order.

Cedillo finally understood how he stood with the president when, in late July and early August of 1937, he tried unsuccessfully to force the president to support him publicly in a confrontation with students of the Agricultural School of Chapingo. Cárdenas was in the Yucatán when Cedillo asked him for support against the students. In an exchange of telegrams, the president chose to accept Cedillo's resignation. Cedillo, who had not actually resigned, was shocked. Perhaps he had threatened to resign if the president did not support his actions, but sources are unclear about this. Returning shortly thereafter to his home state, the caudillo found that locally stationed federal troops surrounded the state capital of San Luis Potosí. More troops soon arrived to squash any armed revolt. Although confrontations between Cárdenas's troops and Cedillo supporters erupted with resulting bloodshed on both sides, Cedillo still had not officially broken with Cárdenas.

Cárdenas next included Cedillo in his plan to separate those caudillos who were military officers from their local power bases by ordering them transferred to other postings. On April 5, 1938, the Secretary of Defense (Secretario de la Defensa Nacional) ordered Cedillo to transfer from San Luis Potosí to Michoacán, the president's home state. The order was routed through General Manuel Avila Camacho, who commanded Cárdenas's troops in San Luis Potosí. Cedillo responded by informing Avila Camacho that he had a hernia and could not travel. Avila Camacho replied that when Cedillo returned to San Luis Potosí, he was automatically returned to active army duty and must obey the order to transfer. Cedillo informed Cárdenas that his hernia was too painful to resume duties as an active duty general, so he requested a complete separation from the army. He told Cárdenas, "I do not desire to intervene in any political matter, wishing to dedicate myself to agriculture at my ranch."[32] Shortly thereafter, Cárdenas released Cedillo from the army, ending his military career permanently.[33]

Cedillo, however,was unwilling to be pushed aside in his home state. He and his supporters planned to launch a rebellion by May 5, 1938, if he was not allowed to continue his influence in shaping state government. The launch date passed; Cedillo still hoped that Cárdenas would relent and allow him to control San Luis Potosí. There matters stood until Cárdenas traveled to San Luis Potosí on May 17.

While the confrontation between Cárdenas and Cedillo developed during 1937 and 1938, the Departamento Confidencial played a significant role in all of Cárdenas's efforts to eliminate uncooperative regional caudillos such as Cedillo and push through reforms. The Army Intelligence Service, which apparently operated independently of other agencies and did not share its information with civilians, also probably monitored Cedillo's activities. Beginning early in 1937, the Departamento Confidencial had informed Cárdenas in detail about the potential for a Cedillo-led insurrection, and well before the actual rebellion agents reported that Cedillo planned to lead the revolt from San Luis Potosí. According to their reports, a local army commander had encountered and briefly skirmished with a group of heavily armed agraristas. The commander claimed that Cedillo had sent these fighters with six machine guns to confront his government troops. The army was similarly armed and prepared to combat any rebels roaming the region.[34] However, no one seemed to know if an armed clash actually occurred, or if all of this was only rumor promoted by the cardenistas. Army leaders reportedly had a list of ten generals who supported Cedillo and another list of local Cedillo supporters who were connected to the petroleum industry. These findings, among others, led agents to conclude that Cedillo and his supporters posed a legitimate threat to the national regime.

As Cárdenas parried with the cedillistas, Ignacio García Tellez, Secretary of Gobernación, clarified the operation of the Departamento Confidencial, now officially called the Department of Political and Social Investigations (Departamento de Investigaciones Políticas y Sociales). He demanded complete reports from agents and accurate descriptions of the attitude of the population toward the government and Cedillo. The Cárdenas government reiterated that the agency should conduct investigations into any organization, person, or activity that might have political or social impact in the country. This extended the agency's assignment to include everything from drug dealing to murder for hire.[35]

On March 18, 1938, when Cárdenas nationalized the petroleum industry in Mexico, a groundswell of support for him arose throughout the country, strengthening his position against Cedillo and other enemies. Cárdenas used this outburst of support to reorganize the PNR. The new political party would be named the PRM (Partido de la Revolución Mexicana), and it included four sectors: labor, agrarian, popular, and military. This reorganization further consolidated Cárdenas's control of the government, and it may have factored in Cedillo's decision to lead an armed rebellion before the president was too powerful to challenge.

On May 15, 1938, Cedillo mobilized approximately fifteen hundred of his loyal supporters in preparation for a full-scale revolt. By this time he probably realized he could not win an armed struggle, but he may have hoped that other state caudillos would join in his rebellion. When Cedillo learned that Cárdenas would visit San Luis Potosí, he hoped that the president would appease him and leave him in charge of his fiefdom. The president had no such intention. Cárdenas surely made this trip as a consequence of reports by the Departamento Confidencial concerning Cedillo's lingering popularity in the state and his recent maneuverings. On May 18, Cárdenas, speaking publicly to workers and agraristas in San Luis Potosí, promised more land redistribution and assistance to workers, and ordered Cedillo to meet with him. He soon learned that Cedillo had already retreated to a rural area. From this outpost Cedillo listened to Cárdenas's speech on the radio, and called for the rebellion to begin. The insurrection that followed was met with increasing numbers of government soldiers sent to reinforce army troops already in place. As more government troops poured in, many of Cedillo's partisans abandoned the cause and returned to their homes. Soon, he had only a few remaining loyal supporters, too few to challenge the government.

Despite Cedillo's flight from the state capital, Cedillo supporters in his home state and in many other areas continued to hope he would eventually succeed. Individuals in many areas continued to plan organized resistance to the government, which remained extremely wary of potential revolts. Agents of the Departamento Confidencial monitored rumored threats throughout the country and along the international border with the United States. This preoccupation with rebel activity likely contributed to one of the agency's difficulties during the period. Field agents reported on anti-regime activities, but seldom included remarks about political corruption. They tended to report only what they considered the most significant developments in a location.

To address this problem, after the middle 1930s the agency required agents to follow a specific format when reporting. For example, when agent Francisco Urrutia traveled to Hermosillo, Sonora, in late summer of 1938 to report on cedillista activities, the agency had given him a form with specific questions he was required to answer. There is little doubt that the agent's answers on the form were subjective, but at least the agency had some method of controlling the type of information gathered. The form included a request for information about the political situation in Sonora, including the names of the individuals who held public office; the primary political problem at the moment; and how the people viewed the national government, the Cedillo rebellion, and the progress of the Revolution. The form also included specific questions about who opposed the national government, who was armed with enough weapons to be a threat, the economic and social conditions of the region, the number of labor organizations and their activities, whether the ejidos were helping the campesinos, the status of government public schools, the jails and their conditions, the number of illegal immigrants in the region, and myriad other items of interest to the central government.[36]

Whether these reports helped shape national policy cannot be determined for certain, but they surely contributed to the sometimes paranoid behavior of government officials. In any event, the Departamento Confidencial dedicated considerable resources to monitoring not just political threats to the regime, but other destabilizing factors around the country as well.

As the threat of rebellion in several sections of the country continued to escalate, the Departamento Confidencial sent more agents to the northern frontier to assist in investigations. Among these was agent Francisco Martínez Flores. He had joined the department in January 1938 and already had considerable experience in investigations. His first stop was Nuevo Laredo, Tamaulipas, before traveling to Matamoros. The agent remarked that he did not encounter any outward support for Cedillo along the frontier nor any across the border in Brownsville, Texas. He reported that the authorities in Brownsville were strongly biased against Mexicans and intolerant of any Mexican political activities. As a result, the city had the distinction of having more Mexicans in jail than any other border city.

From Matamoros the agent traveled to Reynosa, near the Texas border, where he joined agent Castro Reina. Together the two men set out to find where members of the Cedillo family supposedly had taken refuge. After locating the Cedillo home, they observed people coming and going, but did not interfere. Some of these individuals were border travelers living in San Antonio, the US center of activities for those who opposed Cárdenas. The agents learned that the Cedillo family had deposited $78,000 in a bank in San Antonio and $9,000 in a bank in Reynosa. They also learned that a German, Ernst von Merck, a naturalized Mexican citizen, traveled from Nuevo Laredo to San Antonio to meet with Nicolás Rodríguez, a Cedillo supporter. Along with San Antonio, the agents identified McAllen, Texas, as a major center of antigovernment activity.

The agents concluded their report by acknowledging the difficulty of learning much more about potential rebellions in Mexico. On the other hand, they said, it was relatively easy to monitor cedillista activity in the United States. Evidently, a group of cedillista supporters met in San Antonio once each week to plan what they would do once in power in Mexico. The US government had ordered local law enforcement leaders to suppress any organizing on United States soil of rebellions against the Mexican government, however, and most Mexicans in San Antonio were not generally supportive of the cedillista rebellion. In some of the city's commercial businesses, in fact, there were large pictures of Cedillo with "Traitor" written on them; other labels included "fascista, ambicioso, desleal, iluso, ignorante y muchas cosas denigrantes" (fascist, ambitious, disloyal, deluded, ignorant, and many denigrating things). Nevertheless, the two agents suggested to the chief of the Departamento Confidencial that the Cedillo house be watched closely, since there was persistent antigovernment activity there. Additionally, they recommended that Mexican authorities take action against the Cedillo supporters in Nuevo Laredo.[37] Ultimately, the agents determined there was potential for additional difficulty in the region, but the opposition posed no immediate threat.

The Departamento Confidencial often sent more than one agent to a region to conduct investigations. Such was the case early in 1938, when agent Francisco Urrutia joined agents already in Nuevo Laredo to gather information about antigovernment movements, including the Cedillo rebellion. Working with US officials in Laredo, he learned that Enrique Jaime Torres, an agent for the Mexican Products Company who sometimes used the name Garrett, was under surveillance by authorities north of the border. He seemed to be extremely friendly with some old revolutionary generals and was possibly in the business of selling arms and ammunition to anyone with money. He might have had ties to General José Gonzalo Escobar's earlier movement against the government, and perhaps ties to the cedillistas. Reportedly, twenty thousand Italian- or Austrian-made rifles, along with considerable ammunition, had arrived near Galveston, Texas, on an Italian freighter and had been clandestinely flown or shipped to cedillistas, escobaristas, or others opposing the government in Mexico. When the chief of the Departamento Confidencial asked the agents what government or police forces existed in Nuevo Laredo to forestall any rebellion, the agents informed him that only three battalions of reserves were present, and these were poorly armed agrarian workers and others with little or no military training. There were slightly over three hundred men on the rolls, along with some local police, but none of these could be deemed sufficient in the face of any organized armed threat. In addition, the local press was not especially favorable to the central government.

Agents of the Departamento Confidencial suggested that the poor economic conditions of campesinos contributed to discontent in the northern states and added to the Cedillo turmoil. Only one large ejido seemed to produce much, and it did not provide the income necessary for all the rural poor to live at any reasonable level of sustenance. The situation was a miserable one for most people, with bad sanitary conditions and disease prevalent. Agents added that tuberculosis was almost endemic in the entire region. There was little work for campesinos, and some each day headed north to the United States or south away from the frontier region.

There were eighty-one cantinas in the region, more than there were public schools. Vice was rampant. The consumption of marijuana and other drugs was considerable, and the number of people in jail for selling drugs was growing daily. Agents discovered that two groups were responsible for much of the sale of heroin, cocaine, and morphine. Principal leaders of the groups included Jesús Hinojosa, nicknamed "La Mancha," who had been killed in Tampico a few days before the agents arrived, and Feliciano Guerra, known as "El Torero," who actually had been the chief of the Safety or Security Commissions (Comisiones de Seguridad). He frequently traveled back and forth from Monterrey to Nuevo Laredo, allegedly picking up and delivering illegal drugs. An agent of the Departamento Confidencial reported rumors that "intellectual directors of these [drug trafficking operations] are the Presidente Municipal, Pablo Peña, and the chief of the local army garrison (Jefe de la Guarnición)." It was also rumored that Jesús E. Garza, a United States citizen, helped distribute the drugs. Authorities on both sides of the international border had arrested Garza several times. He lived in Texas most of the time, but was originally from Piedras Negras. Finally, agents reported a considerable number of the automobiles stolen in San Antonio were evidently brought to Nuevo Laredo en route to markets in the interior of the country.[38]

The Cárdenas government was aware of the illegal drug sales and auto theft but apparently remained more interested in antigovernment activities than in crime along the border. In the middle of 1938, immediately following the investigations in Nuevo Laredo and other nearby areas, the head of the Departamento Confidencial sent agent Urrutia to Tampico, Tamaulipas, to investigate illegal activities, to report about the threat of the Doradas, and to watch the growing cedillista movement. Upon arrival at the port, agent Urrutia learned that local military authorities exercised strict "vigilance" over all hostile or potentially hostile groups, and that Cedillistas had been active in the area.[39] Although this type of information was hearsay, the agent believed it necessary to report everything he learned to his superiors. Again Urrutia worked with another agent, one who was already in Tampico. The two agents usually began their investigations by carefully reading the local newspapers for any public announcements of the cedillistas, and they often randomly interviewed several local individuals. They learned that the Mexican army stationed in the port monitored antigovernment activity, but that the local civilian authorities were not committed to investigating such threats. Rumor in the port city before Cedillo's rebellion had held that Cedillo would begin his uprising during the second half of May and that the Doradas would probably join him. The agents also identified several individuals rumored to be supporting the rebellion. Lic. Jesús Ferral, a prominent local individual, had met with Cedillo many times and was possibly conspiring to join or organize a rebellion. It was also rumored that former general José Santos Moyano, who lived in the American colony, was the local head of the movement and a representative of General Cedillo. Rumors continued to circulate that, along with Nicolás Rodríguez, Cedillo was gathering arms and ammunition and recruiting individuals to join the movement. Furthermore, the agents believed that José Gross, who was a United States citizen, was the intermediary connecting Cedillo, Rodríguez, and US petroleum companies. Before March 18, 1938, and the nationalization of petroleum assets, petroleum company representatives flirted with supporting Cedillo and other conservatives who disapproved of the president's threats against foreign oil interests. After Cárdenas nationalized the industry, many of those tied in some way to the oil companies lobbied for return of the assets or fair payment. Gross, the agents learned, also had spoken with campesinos and employees of the companies hoping to get their support in opposing Cárdenas's programs. According to these sources, the rebels already had plans in place to cut communications with the rest of the country upon the initiation of fighting. All of the individuals mentioned were known to the local military and civilian authorities.[40] As so often happened when a report of this nature was sent to Mexico City, the government issued no specific or immediate response. In instances where President Cárdenas deemed that armed revolt was imminent, however, he sent more federal troops to the region.

Urrutia traveled widely throughout the frontier and did not have a high opinion of government officials he encountered. He said one of the border inspectors in Tijuana was a "coyote" or predator in all ways and dedicated to enriching himself at the expense of the government.[41] He suggested that General Román Yocupicio, governor of Sonora, was dishonest and dictatorial. The agent suggested that the state was rich and large and that the governor controlled the population through violence and intimidation, jailing or threatening any individual or group who opposed him. Yocupicio was of Mayo descent, had fought in the revolution, and was willing to use strongarm tactics. As a consequence, there was no outward movement to rebel against his authority.[42]

Other agents confirmed that not only in Sonora, but in other regions as well, local governors, usually holding the rank of general, intimidated the population sufficiently to control it. Agent Antonio Méndez Corona traveled to Parral, Chihuahua, in August 1938 to analyze the possibility of rebellion against the government. He was following up on rumors that cedillistas or other antigovernment groups were scheming to start a rebellion in the region. The procedure the agent was required to follow in his investigation included reporting his interpretation of the situation, and again completing a form with very specific questions, including who the principal political types were, what posts they held, and how they operated in the region. Méndez Corona reported that the most powerful individual was a deputy to the state congress. Apparently, he was not dedicated to a specific political ideology, but he managed to control the state through his leadership in the state CTM. The agent said this did not cause any problems because of the apparent political inertia of most of the people in Parral. He speculated that the locals appeared indifferent to politics because they feared reprisals. Everyone in the village knew that the local diputado had recently ordered the murders of several citizens who opposed him. [43]

The Departamento Confidencial also appointed some female agents to work the Cedillo investigation, but few actually operated in the field. One who did engage in fieldwork was Amada Bazán Nava, a thirty-eight-year-old woman who replaced Inspector J. Guadalupe Corona Benavides

Headquarters of Calles supporter General Román Yocupicio, 1929.
Arizona Historical Society, Tucson.

on September, 16, 1938. She was already an employee of the agency, having worked in the Central Office before her assignment to field operations. Four days after her appointment, she received an expense advance and a rail pass and was sent to San Luis Potosí.[44] Once there, she requested credentials showing that she was a reporter for the newspaper *El Nacional*. Agent Bazán Nava learned that several people in San Luis Potosí had been carrying on regular correspondence with General Saturnino Cedillo, but that any accurate information about his activities was difficult to obtain. From what she was able to glean, considerable cedillista strength existed in the region, and General Raymundo Pérez Gallardo, chief of the military section at Ciudad del Maíz, believed that his military zone was in need of a widespread organization to monitor the cedillistas at all times. Judging by the scarcity of information he provided, however, the general probably did not cooperate fully with Bazán Nava's questioning. He may have resented being plied by a woman operative, believing a male should occupy such a position, and was possibly looking for a way to get her sent back to Mexico City. She did inform her superior in Mexico City, Cipriano Arriola, that some cattle belonging to Cedillo, his two sisters, and a nephew had been confiscated at the orders of the local Oficina Federal de Hacienda (Federal Treasury Office). Assuming her work in San Luis Potosí was then completed, Bazán Nava awaited another assignment.[45] Arriola, however, shortly informed the agent that her work there was not finished and directed her to continue monitoring cedillista organizational activities. She should, however, travel wherever she needed to follow the trail of rebel activity.

She soon reported that mysterious things were happening at the home of known Cedillo sympathizers in San Luis Potosí. In one instance, she saw a car stop in front of the house; two women got out quickly and hurried inside. Bazán Nava said the two did not "look just right " and she concluded they were actually men dressed as women. She reported that she was trying to learn more about this residence and the meetings that took place there. Local police authorities were aware of the meetings and informed agent Bazán Nava that they, too, were monitoring the activities at the house.

While in the city, she also learned that, according to the state governor, Elena Cedillo had talked to the local military commander about her brother's possible surrender. She feared, however, that he would be killed. The governor of the state and military officials assured her that Cedillo would not be shot before he could surrender. Agent Bazán Nava then traveled briefly around the state of San Luis Potosí and its surrounding areas, during which time she took fourteen photographs of troops and civilians. Most of these were taken in an Italian community two hours from the city of San Luis Potosí. The photos of the Italian community were possibly related to fears that locals supported Cedillo. The photos may also have been prompted by wild rumors of Cedillo attempting an alliance with the fascist states of Italy and Germany.

Upon her return to San Luis Potosí, she interviewed a Cedillo sister who told her that Cedillo would surrender if given safe passage out of Mexico. She claimed her brother was honorable and would do as he agreed. Bazán Nava passed the information on to the governor and military commander in the region, but they did not offer Cedillo any guarantees. The governor and the military authorities did not want to be accused of assisting the rebellion. Cedillo's supporters had also asked the state to provide funds to cover his living expenses once he was north of the international border. No doubt the authorities were even less willing to accede to that request. Soon thereafter

Cedillo's sister left for El Paso, Texas.

Rumors were rampant that, in late December or early January, Cedillo had been seriously wounded in a fight with federal troops. Allegedly a local physician had gone to where Cedillo was hiding and tried to help him, but was hindered by the primitive field conditions. The doctor suggested that Cedillo surrender, and offered to try to arrange this with local civilian and military authorities. Cedillo told the doctor to do as he wished, and Cedillo's son, who was present, agreed that Cedillo's wound was serious. The ensuing negotiations provided no resolution for the ailing general.[46] Agents reported that although the cedillista problem might be reaching a natural end, the ex-general still had considerable support, including some support among the Catholic clergy. The search for Cedillo continued until two supporters finally revealed his location. On January 11, 1939, General Miguel H. Guzmán and his troops found and executed the rebel leader.[47]

Earlier that winter, on November 25, 1938, agent Bazán Nava had requested that she be allowed to return to Mexico City. Arriola ignored her, so Bazán Nava asked again the next day, citing family problems as the reason for her request. The day after that, she was ordered back to the capital. On December 2, 1938, she was assigned to the Mexico City office of the Departamento Confidencial, where she was placed in charge of organizing an office archive. Her fieldwork days were over although she retained the title of Inspector at the Fifth Level.[48] As late as January 1945, she was still employed in the office and had been promoted to Inspector Eighth Level. Whether she occasionally worked outside the office cannot be verified, but at least until 1945 she probably spent most of her time in the agency archive. She no doubt had an important role in organizing the first twenty-three years of documents that were later transferred to the Mexican National Archives.

Agent Francisco Martínez Flores, who joined the Departamento Confidencial at the end of 1937, and who assisted in the investigations of cedillista activities, later investigated corruption and other prevalent problems throughout the country. He was meticulous in completing his reports, including his own opinions and analyses of the political, social, and military conditions of the locations where he was assigned. He quickly became a trusted agent. When he began his career in the agency, he had little training, which was not unusual for agents. Three days after joining the Departamento Confidencial, the new agent received a thirty-day per diem advance amounting to $112.50 pesos and was dispatched to Tabasco. Two days later, he received verbal orders to proceed to Minatitlán, where he was to gather information about rumored illegal activities of the subchief of the Immigration Office (Oficina de Migración) of the port of Veracruz. The port officer had been on duty since November of the previous year. The officer had received the appointment despite the fact that federal authorities had arrested him for stealing funds while he was chief of the same office in Matamoros, Tamaulipas. Apparently, corruption at the local level was so institutionalized as to be an accepted way of life, and the government had simply transferred him without punishment. When the immigration officer went on to embezzle government funds at Veracruz, however, the Departamento agent's report finally prompted his dismissal.[49]

Furthering Cárdenas's consolidation of power at the federal level, of course, continued to be the Departamento Confidencial's primary assignment. After completing his work in Veracruz, Martínez Flores journeyed to Villahermosa, Tabasco, where he passed himself off as a tourist in order to obtain information about political groups battling for control of the state. As in his earlier investigations, his work related to issues of national versus local control and which candidate the locals seemed to support for president in the coming election of 1940. He reported that he had cultivated friendships with diverse people from all social levels and "obtained some interesting information." He learned that Manuel Bartlett Bautista, General Ernesto Aguirre Colorado, and Senator Lic. Francisco Trujillo Gurría had been using the local press to win popular support. Bartlett Bautista was the PNR organizer in Tabasco, but he was using his position to mold the local party into an organization of campesinos, workers, and soldiers over which he could exercise complete control, a move that would enable him to ignore the national party organization and, hence, the national government. Bartlett Bautista was the only candidate to have an organizing committee, but, according to the agent, Trujillo Gurría clearly remained the local favorite.[50] Martínez Flores soon discovered one possible source of Trujillo Gurría's popularity.

Apparently, upon the suggestion of local politicians, the police habitually arrested any campesinos on the street who appeared inebriated. A day later, an individual functioning as an arbitrator would tell the now-sober campesinos that they must sign an agreement to support Trujillo Gurría as a condition of their release. If they refused to sign, they would be fined $50 pesos, a sum none of them had. No one, the agent remarked, remained in jail. He surmised that this might be why the campesinos seemed to be more interested in cockfighting than in local politics. Cockfighting had been outlawed nationally, but it was still a major sport in the region, and the governor and local army commander were its most active participants.[51]

The Cedillo rebellion officially had ended with the death of its leader on January 11, 1939. But Cárdenas faced the possibility of rebellion again that same year as he maneuvered to control the presidential election of 1940. It soon became apparent that he aimed to select who would be the next president via the structure of the PRM. He already had decided to support Manuel Avila Camacho, Secretario de Gobernación, but he faced strong opposition from several organized political sectors, powerful generals, and some former Calles supporters. The three major contenders were General Juan Andreu Almazán, a popular and wealthy officer in Nuevo León; General Joaquín Amaro, a former Callista; and General Francisco J. Múgica, governor of Cárdenas's home state of Michoacán. All three had the support of conservative business elites, Catholic Church leaders, some groups in the labor and agricultural sectors, and others in the upper classes. These same groups opposed the left-leaning programs of the president.

Cárdenas began his efforts on behalf of Avila Camacho by making several trips to Nuevo León and other states in the frontier during early 1939, hoping to solidify his position and strengthen his influence by promising campesinos more land and loans for their agricultural pursuits—all part of his strategy to tie the aspiring lower classes to the national government.

On most of these trips, agents of the Departamento Confidencial traveled with Cárdenas to gather information about the local political and social conditions. The president specifically wished to talk with General Juan Andreu Almazán. Although Cárdenas had not yet formally announced that he would press for Avila Camacho's selection as the candidate of the PRM, during 1939 and 1940 Almazán's supporters moved ahead and organized a new party to promote Almazán's candidacy. Called the Revolutionary National Unification Party (Partido Revolucionario de Unificación Nacional, or PRUN), it included individuals who had also founded the conservative

National Action Party (Partido Acción Nacional, or PAN).

General Joaquín Amaro's supporters had meanwhile taken steps to organize a conservative, strongly anti-Communist political party to support his candidacy. On December 8, 1938, General Manuel Pérez Treviño in Coahuila condemned the social and political policies of the Cárdenas government and called for the formation of the Revolutionary Anti-Communist Party (Partido Revolucionario Anti-Comunista, or (PRAC).[52] Amaro became the presidential candidate of this party.

The third major candidate, General Francisco Múgica, was a close confidant of Cárdenas, and during 1939, when he realized Cárdenas supported Avila Camacho for the position, he ended his campaign.

Cárdenas, of course, was aware of this political activity on the part of Amaro and Almazán. At the end of April 1939, Cárdenas traveled to Nuevo León in a special railroad car with one additional coach to accommodate some of his entourage. Others of the official party drove by car, allowing them to pass through villages that were not on the rail line. Agents of the Departamento Confidencial continued to provide Cárdenas with a more complete understanding of the problems of the frontier. During this trip, agent Franciso Urrutia was in the official party, and he filed daily reports with his office about presidential activities. Occasionally another agent would briefly join the party, possibly to relay information to Cárdenas.

On April 29, 1939, Cárdenas and his entourage arrived at Monterrey, Nuevo León, where the government was constructing a large irrigation network. The president was received with a considerable show of affection. General Anacleto Guerrero, governor of the state, served as his guide during this part of the trip. That evening, Cárdenas met with General Juan Andreu Almazán at Almazán's ranch. Cárdenas clearly trusted Almazán, because only four others accompanied him. The group spent the night at the ranch. An agent of the Departamento Confidencial reported this meeting to his chief but added that he did not know what was discussed. The next day Cárdenas rejoined his official party, traveling on to Saltillo, Coahuila, where he met with official commissions and other groups to discuss local concerns. Campesinos and others arrived in Saltillo to see Cárdenas and talk personally with him about local problems. The president met with all who came to see him, listened to their problems, and promised to see what could be done to address their concerns.

After these meetings in Coahuila, Cárdenas traveled to Ciudad Obregón, Sonora, where he met with approximately four thousand members of the Confederation of Mexican Workers (Confederación de Trabajadores de México, or CTM), a labor organization with Communist leanings. This workers' organization, founded by Vicente Lombardo Toledano, enjoyed wide local membership; Cárdenas had promoted it as a counter to CROM early in his presidency. At a Yaqui Indian village, leaders asked the president to increase expenditures for irrigation, help end conflicts between labor groups, and provide government funds to improve roads. Cárdenas promised this group that he would do what he could to get these projects underway and improve water quality in the Yaqui regions.[53] He realized that such expenditures helped to secure the loyalty of the locals to the central government, therefore eroding the power of local leaders while strengthening the national government in Mexico City. Considerable information, including interpretations of the president's responses, became part of the agent's reports of these meetings. Probably most important for the Cárdenas government was the Departamento Confidencial's conclusion that the Yaqui were pleased with Cárdenas's promises.

Cárdenas worked closely with the agents who accompanied his official party, and he often gave them special assignments. Frequently, he sent an agent in advance of his entourage to do some fieldwork so he would be informed of local problems and have time to respond effectively. On one occasion, he sent an agent to Torreón, Coahuila, to report on the political and social climate in the Lagunera region. The agent reported that the Spanish Falange, the right-wing, pro-Axis organization that had its main office in Mexico City, was cooperating with the Sinarquistas. This latter faction was a conservative pro-clerical movement that Gildardo González Sánchez coalesced into a political party in 1940. Its support was centered in the north central regions of the country down to Guanajuato, and the party cooperated with clerics to use church pulpits for their political aims. These groups loudly opposed Cárdenas, his ejido land policy, and his selection of General Manuel Avila Camacho as his successor. The agent concluded that while support existed for the Spanish Falange and the Sinarquistas, it was not broad enough to challenge the workers and campesinos who supported the government. He also reported that "political activities were practically suspended throughout the state." Even the contest for local deputies stirred no interest among the voters. The population seemed generally indifferent to official elections, perhaps because most citizens had no confidence in the veracity of officials and the government.[54]

Another agent later offered additional insight into the political ambience of the northern frontier when he reported from Sonora that the state was large and rich, yet plagued by economic problems. The state's economic base was primarily agricultural in its southern sections, where the Yaqui and Mayo Indians farmed, and in other areas mining was the major enterprise. Mining, however, was in decline, and the state was in desperate financial straits. Although Governor Román Yocupicio had his supporters, the agent believed that considerable dissatisfaction existed in some sections of the state.[55]

During 1939 and 1940, agent Francisco Martínez Flores continued his work on the frontier, particularly in Nuevo León. He apparently carried out his assignments efficiently, if his lengthy reports are any indication. In one investigation, he reported that Miguel Rosas, a Mexican citizen and Monterrey policeman, was jailed in Laredo, Texas, for trafficking in marijuana. The agent did not speculate whether the charges were true or not. Local law enforcement officials in Texas sent Rosas to Houston, where he was then deported to Mexico. The agent also investigated the Italian community in Monterrey, as rumors floated about the city that the community was populated by fascist supporters of Italy and Germany, and perhaps might support opposition to Cárdenas's government. However, he found no specific activity that would threaten the government.[56] Martínez Flores remained in the frontier until the end of the summer, when he returned briefly to Mexico City. His surveillance of the border areas was in response to growing concern about possible Axis activities in the region's somewhat isolated northern reaches, as well as in preparation for the election of 1940, to be held in July.

His activities during 1939 and 1940 were generally identical to any agent who worked throughout the country; however, he occasionally traveled north into the United States to take stock of the activities of Mexicans in exile and Mexican consular representatives. In November and December he returned to the United States. In his report after one such trip, he told his superiors that he was shocked at the "lamentable performance of consular agents, who thus reflected poorly upon Mexico." He believed that the consuls were supposed to protect the rights of Mexicans in the United States, but his observations were that in Texas, New Mexico, and Arizona these agents did not comply with their instructions. He also reported upon the activities of several former generals living in the United States. He suggested that the Departamento Confidencial expand its activities in the United States, especially in view of the fact that Mexico did not have a Secret Service other than that which existed in the military and the Federal District Police, and the latter organization worked only locally. He also told the chief of the department that he could not operate successfully in the United States when he was given so little funding. He insisted that he and his coworkers should be paid in United States currency and not in pesos. The exchange rate was not favorable, and Mexican pesos were worth considerably less north of the border.[57]

For the most part, Departamento Confidencial agents working north of the international border were monitoring anti-Cárdenas activities within Mexican exile communities. Many exiles who opposed Cárdenas's term as president were against his choosing a successor, for obvious reasons. But the exile community posed no serious threat to the Cárdenas presidency. The most serious potential opposition to Cárdenas was located in Monterrey, in the form of General Alamazán and his supporters.

By late 1939 and early 1940, Almazán had to decide whether he would accept Cárdenas's decision to make Avila Camacho the presidential nominee of the PRM, essentially assuring his election. He chose to run for the office independent of the PRM, though he recognized that the actual election might be little more than a charade. In much of the country rumors were rampant that he would lead a rebellion against the government if Avila Camacho became president. Cárdenas, of course, had anticipated problems not only from Almazán, but potentially from other rejected candidates as well. Thus, during 1939 and 1940, Cárdenas directed Gobernación to dispatch Departamento Confidencial agents not just to Monterrey, but all across the country, wherever the activities of other putative presidential candidates needed to be monitored. After Almazán had formally announced his candidacy, his conservative base of Nuevo León businessmen, large landowners, and industrialists had made him the candidate of the Partido Acción Nacional (PAN). With the support of the Catholic Church and others who did not want any more left-leaning presidential candidates, he was a formidable opponent to Cárdenas's selection.

In 1940, Cárdenas, alarmed at the potential for rebellion by Almazán and his supporters, again traveled to the frontier to talk with Almazán—possibly hoping to discourage him from continuing his candidacy, or worse, leading an armed rebellion against the government. The talks were cordial, but nothing was resolved. During the course of the negotiations, Almazán insisted that he was a reluctant candidate, but Cárdenas still viewed him as a serious threat and kept agents of the Departamento Confidencial in the field to watch his activities.[58] Cárdenas had reason for his concern.

Early in 1940, the Departamento Confidencial sent agent Martínez Flores from Mexico City back to Monterrey to monitor everything that General Almazán did or said. The agent reported that Almazán's rhetoric against Cárdenas was becoming more vitriolic each day. Almazán posed a serious threat because of the strength of his support in the north and elsewhere, his command of well-armed troops loyal to him, and the support of various labor organizations.[59]

Agent Martínez Flores followed Almazán to Nuevo Laredo in May, where he reported that six thousand people awaited the arrival of the general's party. According to Martínez Flores, one man in the crowd pronounced Almazán a "symbol of the Revolution" who was "virile and valiant and above all, patriotic without limits." Another enthusiastic individual explained that the difference between Almazán supporters and those who wanted to place Avila Camacho in the presidency was that Almazán partisans felt "their patriotism in their hearts, while the others felt it in their stomachs. Viva Almazán!" cried the passionate supporter. Upon his arrival, Almazán spoke to the crowd, telling those present that he would go everywhere in the country to campaign. He suggested that those who had selected Avila Camacho were following the pattern of Hitler and Stalin, both of whom represented totalitarian control. Several other Almazán supporters spoke on behalf of their candidate. Agent Martínez Flores reported that the state's governor had organized peaceful protests against Almazán, but it was locally known that he secretly supported the candidate. In the opinion of the agent, however, most ordinary citizens in Nuevo León were indifferent to the presidential selection. As a consequence of such widespread apathy, this agent did not believe it necessary for him to remain in the frontier to watch Almazán supporters.[60]

To Cárdenas and others of the PRM, however, Almazán remained a credible threat, and agents of the Departamento Confidencial continued to investigate all activities that appeared to threaten Camacho's candidacy. They constantly followed and analyzed Almazán's movements.[61] When a few army officers met with Almazán in Mexico City during the fall of 1939, agents reported they had discussed the election and agreed to establish committees in each state to support Almazán. In Veracruz, where General Roberto Fernández Cejudo headed that state's almazanista organization, the investigating agent reported that he had heard Fernández Cejudo say disparaging things about Cárdenas. In fact, his insulting rhetoric had included threats of assassination.[62]

Supporters had staged Pro-Almazán rallies in Mexico City during several months of 1939. One was held in the Alameda de Santa María la Ribera and attracted pro-Avila Camacho individuals, some armed with guns and knives. A scuffle between the groups led to broken glass, shots fired, and, eventually, the arrival of Federal District police to restore order. Agents continued monitoring the Almazán organizers, following them to Veracruz, to the northern frontier, and anywhere else in the country they might find success.

On one occasion, agent Cipriano Arriola reported to the Departamento Confidencial that he had been present in the state of Puebla when Avila Camacho supporters fired shots, threw rocks, and blocked the path of the almazanistas. He also reported that he witnessed state police and other Avila Camacho supporters detain a train. Pro-Avila Camacho people drove vehicles that belonged to the federal Secretariat of Communications (Secretaría de Comunicaciones), indicating, of course, that government funds were being used to support Avila Camacho's candidacy. Several of the almazanistas were wounded when shots were fired; others were injured when the Avila Camacho supporters threw rocks and bottles. Houses and automobiles of the Almazán supporters also suffered damage.[63]

Agents continued to monitor other antigovernment activities throughout the country. José M. Clavé traveled to Monterrey in the middle of the Almazán confrontation to investigate rumors that additional antigovernment elements had formed an armed movement. The agent found that many political groups and agrarian leaders supported Avila Camacho, but at one meeting he heard veteran army officers threaten to raise arms, claiming to be ready to give the Avila Camacho supporters a "bad surprise."[64] Rumors about these movements of the almazanistas were especially rampant on the frontier. Almazán supposedly met with representatives of the Texas Oil Company and Standard Oil when he briefly traveled to San Antonio during the late summer of 1940. Agents of the Departamento Confidencial heard this but could not verify whether the trip actually had occurred.[65]

When the government announced that Avila Camacho had won the presidential election, Almazán chose to distance himself from any rebellion against the government. After some thought, he apparently concluded that it might cost him more than he could gain. In fact, as voter fraud was common in elections, Avila Camacho may not have won the votes to be president, but he was the choice of the PRM and Cárdenas, which was sufficient. Almazán remained loyal to the regime. Cárdenas's success in institutionalizing the process of choosing a president through the governing political party established a pattern in Mexican politics that lasted several decades.

Throughout the Almazán affair and after, agents of the Departamento Confidencial continued to monitor the general political ambience in the country. During 1940, agent Jesús González Valencia, working in Coahuila, reported that there were still thousands of individuals in that state who would support Almazán. He informed his superiors that he was prolonging his visit by fifteen days in order to complete his analysis of the Almazán movement and other political matters. Additional agents also monitored labor and political activities in the northern frontier.

As the election process had proceeded , and finally ended, agent José M. Clavé had continued to scrutinize activities in Saltillo, Coahuila. Although the Communist Party there had an active organization that included students, some middle-class individuals, and various political failures, pro-Avila Camacho partisans continued to control the official government machinery and workers' organizations.[66] By the end of 1940, agents reported from Coahuila and Nuevo León that the locals now seemed somewhat indifferent to electoral activities, including the elections of deputies to state or national government offices.[67] Most probably believed that no matter how they voted, their votes would not be counted fairly. In many respects they understood that they could not control their own political fate.

Local contests, however, could be deadly. Local disputes—as well as a growing concern about the war overseas—placed increasing demands on the agents of the Departamento Confidencial during 1940. In February, agent Erwin Friedeberg, assigned to Acapulco, complained that his workload was excessive. He said he was presently investigating the assassination of a local member of the national Chamber of Deputies. Pronouncing this a politically motivated crime, he added that it would demand considerable time to determine who had been responsible. He also suggested that such crimes were standard fare for the region, no doubt prompted by heated contests for local political offices. In his report he complained that "the quantity of cases to investigate is truly overwhelming." The agent said he personally had heard the gunshots that killed one local politician, Antonio Nogueda Radilla. According to his report, Nogueda Radilla had talked to the agent earlier about some killings in the town and had agreed to talk further with him. Later Friedeberg heard a loud, angry discussion in the hotel room next to his. He realized that one of these individuals was Nogueda Radilla. The agent heard one man insist that Nogueda Radilla leave with him, but Nogueda Radilla refused. More shouting followed, and Nogueda Radilla eventually left with the man. Soon thereafter the agent heard several shots fired. Nogueda Radilla was the only one killed, and the agent believed local police were involved. He concluded in the report to his chief that Guerrero was a dangerous place to live. He said families fought families, and vendettas were common.[68]

World War II had been ongoing in Europe since the German invasion of Poland in September 1939, and in 1940 it loomed as a potential problem for Mexico. Even before the presidency of General Manuel Avila Camacho, the Departamento Confidencial would begin to shift its focus toward investigating international threats to security. By 1941 the Mexican government realized that it would be difficult for Mexico to remain neutral in the war.[69] Although military intelligence also operated in this sphere, monitoring the activities of Axis-connected individuals within Mexico fell to a great extent to the Departamento Confidencial. In addition to its regular activities of keeping track of antigovernment movements and groups, the agency now would be required to watch carefully the actions of all persons with any kind of connection to Germany, Japan, or Italy.[70]

CHAPTER 4

NATIONAL SECURITY AND THE DEPARTAMENTO CONFIDENCIAL, 1940–1946

General Manuel Avila Camacho, who assumed the presidency of Mexico December 1, 1940, was born in Teteles, Puebla, near the border with Veracruz, in 1896. He inherited from Lázaro Cárdenas a tense situation between Mexican capital and labor that was a direct result of the former president's leftist programs. Beginning in 1913, Avila Camacho had fought with the Constitiutionalist forces of Venustiano Carranza in several major battles during the struggle against General Victoriano Huerta. He later became a loyal supporter of General Cárdenas. After Cárdenas became president, he appointed Avila Camacho Secretario de la Defensa Nacional, where he had considerable influence in continuing the professionalization of the Mexican military. Avila Camacho, by nature a conciliator, sought to avoid personal conflict whenever possible. Nevertheless, his administration, along with World War II, changed the country, and to a considerable extent the focus of the Departamento Confidencial.

The new president immediately signaled to all political sectors and organizations that he was more a political centrist than an extreme right- or left-wing zealot. Avila Camacho's administration was more conservative than any since revolutionary fighting had ceased, however. Soon after assuming office, Avila Camacho removed from governmental positions most of the remaining leftists from the Cárdenas presidency. His administration backed away from the socialist model that supported rapid agrarian reform and ended other leftist policies of the Cárdenas era. His philosophy toward business and his overall conservatism led him to abandon the large-scale land reform initiatives that Cárdenas had championed. Avila Camacho's announcement that he was a "believer" signaled that he would seek continuing reconciliation between the government and the Catholic Church. Wealthy conservative businessmen throughout the country, initially somewhat wary, eventually accepted him, believing he would direct the country away from

En proceso de catalogación: Manuel Avila Camacho becomes president. With him are former presidents, beginning second from left: Pascual Ortiz Rubio, Abelardo Rodríguez, Plutarco Elías Calles, Avila Camacho at microphone, Lázaro Cárdenas, Emilio Portes Gil. Fideicomiso Archivos Plutarco Elías Calles y Fernando Torreblanca. México, DF.

cardenista politics. After some consideration, the economically powerful Monterrey business group supported him in the presidential election over local conservative General Juan Andreu Almazán. During Avila Camacho's administration, Mexico became increasingly involved in international affairs, and the government firmly allied itself with business and economic development elites. Social and political changes, along with the prospect of the war in Europe reaching Mexico, led to improved diplomatic, political, and business relations with the United States. The Mexican military also made command and matériel changes to prepare for any national security threats posed by the conflagration that was beginning to engulf most of the world.[1]

During his presidency, Avila Camacho renewed diplomatic relations with the Soviet Union and Great Britain, devoted more money to improving education, created Mexican Social Security (1943), slowly broadened the ejidal system that Cárdenas had promoted, supported a new electoral law regulating political parties, favored expansion and consolidation of private

On the right, Lázaro Cárdenas; standing next to him is Maximino Avila Camacho, the president's brother.
Archivo General De La Nación, México, DF.

banking, and promoted various other changes that affected the country's economy and governance. He modernized Mexico's economy by promoting private industry and devaluing the currency to obtain better international trade agreements. He also favored civilian over military leadership, appointing civilians rather than army officers to important positions in government. His administration reorganized the governing political party, the PRM (Partido de la Revolución Mexicana). In 1946, the party name changed to Partido Revolucionario Institucional (Institutional Revolutionary Party, or PRI), and the military was officially omitted from party sector organization.

Significant changes were also occurring throughout the world. In 1933, seven years before the election of Avila Camacho, Franklin D. Roosevelt became president of a United States deeply mired in economic depression. He promised the American people a "New Deal" to resolve the economic crisis that was triggered by the stock market crash of 1929. By 1933, the depression had spread throughout much of the world. Roosevelt's New Deal programs

President Manuel Avila Camacho (right) with his brother Maximino.
Archivo General De La Nación, México, DF.

addressed, but did not resolve, the suffering that the depression had caused. Domestic issues consumed most of Roosevelt's attention until it was clear that international problems might present an even greater threat to security.

In Germany, the rise to power of Adolf Hitler and the National Socialist German Workers' Party (NSDAP), or Nazis, was nearly simultaneous with Roosevelt's presidential inauguration. Economic depression in Germany that worsened monthly had contributed to Hitler's growing power. The Nazis soon embarked on a plan to address the depression and to restore the nation to what Hitler saw as a glorious German past that had been squandered in the post–World War I period. He planned to rearm Germany, make it a first-rate military power, and then expand its borders until a new German Reich encompassed a large section of Western Europe.

In 1936, as General Francisco Franco, a right-wing army officer, led a revolt against the republican government of Spain, Hitler's Luftwaffe (air force) refined its tactics in that country by flying missions against Spanish republican forces. With German air support, advisers, and ammunition, Franco's forces established control of the country. By early 1938, Hitler had rearmed Germany, reestablished hegemony over areas in the Rhineland that

Germany had lost after World War I, and annexed Austria. In 1938, he bullied Czechoslovakia into surrendering a German-speaking area of its territory referred to as the Sudetenland, annexing the rest of the country the next year. In 1939, he sent the Wehrmacht (army) to attack Poland from the west as Soviet leader Josef Stalin sent his forces to attack from the east. Besieged from both sides, Poland quickly succumbed to German and Soviet military might. The invasion of Poland finally elicited a reaction from British leader Neville Chamberlain, who had guaranteed Polish sovereignty. Britain soon thereafter entered the war against the Nazis. The next year Hitler sent the Wehrmacht into France, quickly defeating that country. In 1941, although many of his goals had been attained, Hitler's eastward expansion suffered a setback when he decided to attack the Soviet Union. An exceedingly harsh winter caused German troops to lose initiative, and they were ultimately forced to withdraw, sustaining huge losses in men and matériel.

On December 7, 1941, the United States was shaken from its 1920s pacifism when a Japanese carrier-based air fleet attacked the United States naval facilities at Pearl Harbor, Hawaii. The Japanese surprise attack destroyed or disabled several United States Pacific fleet battleships in a two-hour air raid that killed more than two thousand individuals and wounded several hundred more. This action provoked the United States to declare war against both Japan and Germany. Hitler had already declared war against the United States. By the time of this attack, the United States had inherited an unlikely ally in the Soviet Union.

The deteriorating world situation during the 1930s provides an historical context for American hemispherical relations, especially diplomacy between the United States and Mexico. In 1938, President Lázaro Cárdenas nationalized United States and other foreign oil assets in Mexico, temporarily creating international tension between Mexico and several other countries. By this time, FDR had attempted through diplomacy to halt the aggression of Germany and Japan. With the two powers refusing to abandon their expansionism, Roosevelt realized that he must address tensions with Mexico and establish the countries' mutual cooperation should the war in Europe or Asia expand into the western hemisphere. He also worked to improve relations with the rest of Latin America through his hemisphere-wide Good Neighbor Policy.[2]

In his first term as president, Roosevelt's administration officially denounced the United States' historical interference in the internal or external affairs of Latin American nations. In 1933, at a hemispheric conference in Uruguay, the United States informed other North and South American nations that it would withdraw its troops from Haiti and the Dominican Republic. Perhaps the most successful outcome of the policy was that the United States did not intervene when Mexico nationalized petroleum production, except to insist that petroleum companies receive a fair settlement for their investments. Between 1938 and 1940, FDR successfully negotiated a final settlement between American oil companies and the Mexican government regarding ownership rights of the petroleum industry in Mexico.

While the Good Neighbor Policy helped pave the way for improved relations, it did not signal the end of the United States' meddling in other nations' economies, nor did it stop Washington's financial and military aid to right-wing dictators who were establishing powerful regimes in several countries. Overall, however, and despite some backsliding on the part of Washington, relations in the hemisphere slowly improved during this critical time of German and Japanese expansion.

Despite continued tensions, by the time Avila Camacho assumed the presidency of Mexico, internal political unrest in the country had generally subsided. Economic conditions were also slightly improved, as were relations with the United States. As president, Avila Camacho enthusiastically encouraged foreign investment in Mexico and believed that to win the confidence of foreign investors, the government had to provide guarantees that they would not lose their investments through government actions. The new president also sided with businesses against labor interests. He returned some formerly confiscated lands to previous owners, especially in the Yucatán, and made it clear that agrarian reform would not be the main focus of his administration.

Avila Camacho was the first president since General Porfirio Díaz to openly support the Catholic Church.[3] He systematically purged leftists from government education agencies, directing education toward the center-right politically. He also used the powers of his office to limit the activities and influence of the Mexican Communist Party (Partido Comunista Mexicano, or PCM). These changes were part of an ongoing ideological battle, and

Avila Camacho's appointment of his older brother Maximino as Secretario de Comunicaciones y Obras Públicas (Secretary of Communications and Public Works) may also have been motivated by his move to the right. This ill-conceived appointment, however, provided additional opportunities for Maximino, referred to by many as "Mr. Fifteen Percent," to continue his policies of graft and intimidation, practices he had perfected during his years as governor of Puebla, where he demanded a fifteen percent cut of any profits from businesses under his purview. Leaders of the Confederation of Mexican Workers (Confederación de Trabajadores de Mexico, or CTM), who had supported Manuel Avila Camacho for president, were not pleased with the appointment of Maximino, or with several of the new president's other changes.

Avila Camacho revealed his more conservative tendencies soon after taking power when he sent police units to break up workers' demonstrations and strikes in the Federal District. On several occasions, mounted police beat, wounded, or killed striking CTM workers. Facing the strong opposition of the government, the CTM declined in influence while the Regional Confederation of Mexican Workers (Confederación Regional Obrera Mexicana, or CROM) once again increased its power. His conservative attitude toward labor led Avila Camacho to ignore right-wing violence against labor unions and their members.

Despite the period's social and political changes, Avila Camacho somehow avoided a split in the Mexican Revolutionary Party (Partido de la Revolución Mexicana, or PRM). The party assumed a centrist political stance and, by seeking middle ground, was able to control the country without great difficulty. Avila Camacho no doubt profited politically from World War II, since the war made it easier to direct the country back toward a more pro-business and conservative economic, social, and political posture.

Throughout the 1930s, right-wing political groups such as the Sinarquistas, Doradas, and Spanish Falange, all of which leaned toward European fascism, had posed a potential threat to the PRM and, arguably, to the Cárdenas regime. In the early 1940s, these groups still had significant numbers of followers. The Falange was the pro-fascist party in Spain that put General Franciso Franco in power and ended democratic participation in government. Although President Avila Camacho tolerated right-wing opposition for most of World War II, on June 23, 1944, he outlawed the Sinarquistas. For the most part, however, the various right-wing groups posed no serious threat to the Avila Camacho regime, as they were too far on the fringe of Mexican political life to win broad support. Once the war began, these elements were further relegated to the periphery, for they appeared to the average Mexican to be pro-fascist.

Mexico's entrance into World War II initiated changes for all political and economic sectors in the country. It also prompted a broadening of the duties of the Departamento Confidencial and its chief, José Lelo de Larrea Domínguez, to include monitoring the activities of German, Japanese, or Italian residents. Internal espionage included monitoring people born in these countries who had either acquired Mexican citizenship or lived in the country for many years. Axis diplomats and businessmen also fell under the department's surveillance. Mexican authorities feared sabotage of petroleum facilities and other industries providing raw materials for the war effort. In fact, many national deputies proposed that Japanese in Mexico either be expelled or imprisoned in camps.

The agency continued its duties as before, but received more funding and became more important in the bureaucracy. It continued observation of political and social activities, as it had done for years, but most of its resources were dedicated to the potential problems the war or Axis-related individuals might cause.[4] As the central government had become stronger, there were fewer homegrown threats to monitor.

When World War II began, Mexico supported the Allied cause by breaking diplomatic relations with Axis countries, but it did not officially enter the war until May 1942, when a German submarine torpedoed a Mexican freighter in the Gulf of Mexico.[5] The more than six-thousand-ton government-owned Mexican oil tanker Potrero del Llano, plying through the Gulf of Mexico and carrying 37,358 barrels of crude oil to the United States, sank with the loss of fourteen sailors out of the ship's complement of thirty-five. The Mexican government bitterly reminded Germany that Mexico was a neutral country, that the ship had its lights on, and that it was flying the Mexican flag. The vessel previously had been the Italian ship Lucifero, but Mexico confiscated it in 1940 because Mussolini had refused to pay petroleum debts. On May 21, a little more than a week after this first attack, a German submarine torpedoed and destroyed a second Mexican oil tanker, the Faja de Oro, also in the Gulf. Seven of the twenty-eight crewmen died, while six were wounded or badly burned. This ship also had been sailing with all lights on and flying the Mexican flag. It was another old Italian vessel, the Genoano, confiscated in retaliation for Italian debts owed the Mexican government.[6] The vessel's tanks were empty, but fumes caused a secondary explosion. The submarine then fired on rescue ships, sinking one.

The sinking of the second Mexican tanker elicited even stronger reactions from Mexicans, many calling for war against Germany. Angry university students attacked the German Club in Mexico City, breaking windows and causing other damage.[7] Although many Mexicans remained committed to staying out of the war at any cost, on May 22, 1942, Avila Camacho led his country in a declaration of war against Germany and its Axis partners, stating that there was no other recourse for Mexico. Mexico's declaration of war prompted the Departamento Confidencial to increase the number of agents and its surveillance of Axis-related individuals in the country. Operatives who were sent to monitor labor activities and demonstrations were advised to look for any Axis leanings expressed in these gatherings.

Soon after the sinking of the first Mexican oil tanker, some Mexicans called for the immediate confinement of Germans, Italians, and Japanese who lived in the country. Many angry Mexicans also demanded the expropriation or freezing of assets of companies in Mexico that Axis nationals owned or controlled. One senator remarked that the Mexican government should place in concentration camps all persons living in Mexico who were citizens of Axis nations or of German, Italian, or Japanese descent, and require them to work as compensation for the damages caused by the German submarines. Many Mexicans shared this sentiment and believed that their government should go beyond simple relocation or confinement. These citizens demanded the immediate arrest of all persons with Axis sympathies living in the country.[8] Ultimately, Mexican authorities chose only to relocate people who had some connection with the Axis nations, and while this created considerable hardships on the individuals, it was not as drastic as the policy followed in the United States.

The difficulties encountered by the government with respect to Axis-connected people in the country can only be fully understood in the context of Mexican immigration, United States–Mexico relations, and issues between Cárdenas and Axis nations during the late 1930s.

On March 18, 1938, when Cárdenas nationalized the Mexican petroleum industry, he created a serious conflict with the United States. The United States oil companies owned facilities and had titles to subsoil rights in Mexico. After nationalization, these companies pressured the United States government to establish an oil embargo against Mexico, thereby limiting Mexico's ability to sell its crude. While an embargo was imposed on the big oil companies, it did not seriously injure Mexico, for Pemex sought and quickly secured other markets for its petroleum.[9] Germany, Japan, and Italy were part of this new market. These countries were rapidly creating strategic petroleum reserves to support their imperialist agendas. Germany, with its long tradition of business investment in Mexico, was most aggressive in buying Mexican crude. Between mid-1938 and December of 1941, Mexican oil exports to Germany amounted to 48% of the country's total exports. Italy received 17%, the United States 20% (by means other than the large oil companies), and Japan bought a lesser percentage.[10]

Roosevelt's eventual agreement with Mexico regarding petroleum assets was not what the oil companies in the United States had demanded. However, given the growing likelihood of US involvement in the war, FDR had been willing to settle the dispute without Mexican concessions. Through his creation of the Good Neighbor Policy and his attendance at Pan American Conferences in Buenos Aires (1936), Lima (1938), Panama (1940), and Havana (summer of 1940), Roosevelt had shown that the United States desired to improve bilateral relations with Latin America in general, and Mexico in particular. In strengthening relations between the United States and other nations in the hemisphere, the president clearly aimed to create a united front to Axis aggression.

Presidents Cárdenas and Avila Camacho recognized by 1934 that there were fascist fifth column operatives in Mexico, and both vigorously opposed this interference in Mexico's internal affairs. They had ordered the Departamento Confidencial to compile detailed files describing the activities of the Spanish Falange and the Sinarquistas in Mexico and documenting their relationship to the Nazis.[11] In addition to monitoring these groups, the agency intensified its efforts to scrutinize the activities of all resident foreigners.

After Hitler's rise to power, Germans in Mexico were the most visible and active fascists. Many were wealthy and had sought to reawaken German nationalism among Germans living abroad. The Mexican government, using the Departamento Confidencial and military intelligence, rapidly compiled case files on German activities. To the chagrin of Mexican authorities, the Nazi government had encouraged Germans to send their children to German schools (only pure Aryans could attend) and had suggested that their parents join German associations in Mexico City. They also established a Hitler Youth organization in the Mexican Federal District and distributed propaganda throughout the country to convince Mexicans to remain neutral in the event that the United States entered the war against Germany. Furthermore, because Germany recognized dual citizenship, the German consulate suggested that Germans living in Mexico become Mexican citizens. As dual citizens, they could better protect themselves and their assets in the event of war.

In December 1940, after his election to an unprecedented third term as president of the United States, FDR became so concerned about Mexico's relationship with Axis nations that he dispatched Vice President Henry A. Wallace to Mexico City to represent the United States at the inauguration of Manuel Avila Camacho. Roosevelt also instructed Wallace to approach Avila Camacho about the creation of a joint hemispheric defense committee (accomplished in early 1942) in the event that the United States entered the war. Mexican authorities were receptive to the suggestions, just as they had earlier responded to Nazi expansion in Europe by supporting the Spanish Republic during the Spanish Civil War. In 1939, Cárdenas had indicated to FDR that Mexico, neutral in the war that began that year in Europe, opposed any country interfering in the internal affairs of smaller or weaker countries. Therefore, Mexico officially opposed Germany's interventionist policies and its annexation or invasion of neighboring European countries. Shortly after the inauguration, however, Avilo Camacho informed the United States that he would cooperate in eliminating the influence in Mexico of German, Italian, and Japanese individuals and companies, but that Mexico was not yet willing to abandon officially its neutral stance.

The Director of the Departamento Confidencial assigned several agents to investigate Nazi activity in Mexico City in 1940. These agents were identified only by number, and the numbers changed constantly.

Their investigations were thorough, and the completed reports–some almost thirty pages long–were divided into sections detailing internal organization, propaganda, espionage, subversive activities, financing, reorientation of activities as a consequence of the war, and a few additional considerations. The agents reported that upon Adolf Hitler's ascension to power in 1933, Germany immediately sought to influence or control all Germans, including those living in foreign countries, whether naturalized in that country or not. Agents reported that Nazi propaganda activities had begun in Mexico during this early period, and by 1935, Gestapo operatives using the German Embassy as a base expanded efforts among Germans in Mexico, creating the Popular German Community (La Comunidad Popular Alemana), a political organization for German workers in Mexico; a Hitler Youth Organization; and other groups that would bring Germans in Mexico under the umbrella of the Third Reich. Such activities were frequently financed through both voluntary and forced contributions from German businesses operating in Mexico, as well as by funds from wealthy German residents.

According to the agents, during the early and middle 1930s, Germans attached to the German legation organized both covert and overt activities on behalf of the Nazi government. Dr. Heinrich Northe, officially the First Secretary of the German legation in Mexico City, secretly operated as the supreme authority controlling Nazi activities of all types in the country. Agents continuously monitoring his activities reported that Northe had made several trips to San Luis Potosí to talk with Cedillo and to Sonora to talk with General Román Yocupicio. The German Ambassador, Barón Ruedt von Collenberg, generally refrained from participating directly in Nazi activities, but he did hold banquets for Mexican army generals, journalists, and other groups, obviously hoping to cultivate support for Germany among these important individuals. Some Mexican agents thought von Collenberg was in fact the Gestapo chief for Mexico. Arthur Dietrich, also attached to the embassy, was described as an unscrupulous individual with a criminal record who was the head of the Nazi propaganda effort. Agents further indentified Margot Trauwitz, Mexican by birth but of German ancestry and educated in Germany, and Wilhelm Wirtz, a German national, as dedicated Nazi ideologues and leaders of Nazi organizational efforts in Mexico.

The Departamento Confidencial concluded that La Comunidad Popular

Alemana in Mexico was the center of gravity for all Nazi social clubs and recreational activities and for all so-called racially pure Germans. It was clear that these Nazis did not recognize German Jews and other non-Aryans as German citizens, and these Germans were not included. All of these organizations were obligated to provide financial contributions to the German effort in Mexico, but in the opinion of the Mexican agents, Dietrich pocketed much of this money. Further assisting the Nazi effort in Mexico were old German organizations such as El Casino Alemán (The German Club), as well as the Hitler Youth organization. Each Sunday, these Aryan youths practiced marching to encourage devotion and duty to Germany. El Colegio Alemán (The German School) had about three hundred students, and between 1933 and 1940 it graduated about two thousand "racially pure" students.

The Departamento Confidencial also scrutinized the German business community, reporting that it was influential in assisting the Nazis, and that most of these companies complied with the Nazi decree to hire only racially pure Germans. These companies dispensed propaganda, contributed money to the Nazi cause, and encouraged the Mexican government to allow more German Aryan workers and commercial agents to immigrate to Mexico. These recent arrivals to the country met at the Hotel Reforma or Hotel Ritz and talked with other Germans. They seemed to have considerable money, but it appeared they did nothing to earn this cash. Although some of these individuals doubtless were what they claimed to be, Mexican agents concluded most were probably German agents, either Gestapo or from one of the other German intelligence agencies.

Finally, agents reported that while it was easy to obtain information on most foreign organizations in Mexico—someone was always willing to talk freely about their activities—the Germans were far less forthcoming. Usually, they would not talk to anyone outside the German community. Even those Germans who were anti-Nazi feared to violate this code, believing that someday the Nazis might control Mexico and pursue informers. The agents of the Departamento Confidencial believed that Nazis in Mexico were a genuine threat to the country and every means should be employed to curtail their activities.[12] However, according to Friedrich Schuler, who has researched Mexican and German documents carefully, the United States FBI and British Secret Service had been systematically destroying the German espionage network in Mexico for some time. The wartime threat to Mexico may have been less substantial than Departamento Confidencial agents believed.[13]

Japanese presence in Mexico, especially on the west coast and the Baja California peninsula, also concerned the Mexican government. For several decades, Japanese fishermen had fished along most of the west coast of Mexico. In 1940, before Mexico officially entered the war, a Mexican navy patrol had forced a Japanese fishing boat to land at Acapulco, supposedly for taking depth soundings near the ports. The Japanese, however, claimed they were only looking for fish. As Mexico was not then at war with Japan, the Japanese minister to Mexico soon secured the release of the boat and its crew.

Some Japanese in Mexico lived near the United States border. These Japanese engaged in agriculture or owned small businesses, and a few worked in various professions. Japanese were also located in other parts of the country, many in Chiapas, some residing on the coast of Mexico near Veracruz, and others scattered throughout the country.[14]

By early 1940, the United States Federal Bureau of Investigation, under direction of the tyrannical and paranoid J. Edgar Hoover, had several operatives working in Mexico to report the activities of Axis agents. One individual that the United States sent to Mexico was Gus T. Jones, a veteran FBI agent who had served in Mexico from time to time, over a period of many years. The FBI sent him to the United States embassy in Mexico City as a civilian attaché, although the Mexicans were aware that he was one of Hoover's operatives. Jones worked with agents of Gobernación and members of other Mexican government agencies charged with keeping track of Axis agents and their subversive activities.[15] Although much of the information supplied to Hoover and passed on to the Mexican government and to the United States Department of State was inaccurate, Hoover's organization often accurately identified Nazi supporters or agents. For example, the FBI advised the Mexican government that Arthur Dietrich of the German embassy was distributing German propaganda.[16] Mexican officials already knew of Dietrich's operation and, after May 1940, expelled him and a few others engaged in this effort.[17] Mexican leaders were genuinely concerned about the activities of Nazi operatives, and on May 18, 1940, the Mexican president ordered the Secretary of Gobernación, Miguel Alemán Valdés, to locate and detain any Germans who might be engaged in subversion in Mexico.[18]

By 1940, Germany had been sending intelligence experts to Mexico for some time. Admiral W. F. Canaris, chief of the Abwehr, a naval intelligence-gathering agency responsible to the German Military High Command, had dispersed agents throughout Latin America and monthly increased their number by May of 1939. Working alongside but often not cooperating with the Abwehr was the SD (Sicherheitsdienst), the Nazi party's counterintelligence and intelligence agency. Originally under the direction of Reinhard Heydrich, and then under Heinrich Himmler, the SD also worked in the area of foreign intelligence gathering. The Gestapo was a separate organization, but SD operatives often served as Gestapo agents as well. Other Nazi organizations also sent operatives to Latin American countries. As a result, there was no shortage of German agents working in Mexico by 1941. These operatives attempted to identify and foil enemy agents and to mislead special investigators of Gobernación who were charged with keeping track of German espionage activities.[19] The various German agencies were often more involved with intra-Nazi struggles, however, than with carrying on work in the interest of the fatherland.

By December 7, 1941, records of the Departamento Confidencial clearly indicated that Mexican authorities had taken a number of steps to deal with Axis activity in the country. President Avila Camacho had suggested to Secretary Miguel Alemán Valdés that Mexico needed to identify and monitor all individuals of German, Italian, and Japanese ancestry, citizens and resident aliens alike. The Departamento Confidencial was already doing so before Japan's surprise attack on Pearl Harbor, but with the attack, and Roosevelt's immediate declaration of war, the effort intensified. The United States applied more pressure on the Mexican government to stop all Axis activity, and sent to Mexico a blacklist of German, Italian, and Japanese firms and individuals who should be watched, carefully controlled, or deported.

Miguel Alemán Valdés appointed José Lelo de Larrea Domínguez agency chief, ordering him to identify Axis sympathizers to be watched. Furthermore, in the event that Mexico entered the war, the chief was charged with preparing a list identifying individuals for relocation or internment away from the coastal areas. Lelo de Larrea had entered government service for the first time in January 1941 and spoke English and French.[20] Under his wartime leadership, the Departamento Confidencial concentrated on the influence or role of Axis nationals in Mexico. Lelo de Larrea was capable and dedicated to this task, dispatching agents throughout the country to gather information. His appointment also brought a significant funding increase for the agency and an elevated status within the government.

During 1941, German agents entered Mexico by many routes. Several arrived claiming to be refugees from occupied countries; others obtained passports either in Portugal or Spain. A few claimed to be German Jews who escaped the Nazis.[21] Lelo de Larrea and his agents were aware of these methods of illegal entry, and they sought to identify Axis agents as they passed through customs into Mexico.[22]

Almost immediately after the United States' declaration of war on Japan, the Mexican government broke diplomatic relations with the Japanese and froze all Japanese assets and funds in Mexico. On December 11, 1941, after Germany and Italy also declared war on the United States, Mexico broke diplomatic relations with these Axis nations and ordered its representatives in Japan, Germany, and Italy to close their embassies and return home. The next day it froze the assets and funds of all nationals from these countries.[23]

With war raging between the United States and Axis powers, Mexico determined to intensify its surveillance of Axis officials in the country by monitoring more closely their former legation buildings and offices. Mexico also advised all members of the diplomatic legations of Germany, Italy, and Japan that they could not leave Mexico City without prior permission from the Secretary of Foreign Relations (Secretario de las Relaciones Exteriores).[24] In fact, Lelo de Larrea had already sent agents to monitor the daily movements of employees of the various legations and to watch individuals of Axis descent, whether they were known to be pro-Nazi or not. The outbreak of war between the United States and the Axis nations, and Mexico's response, prompted some people of German descent in Mexico City who were members of an organization called the Pro-German Cultural League (La Liga Pro-Cultura Alemana en México) to express their support for Mexico and the democracies by holding a rally on December 12 at a large theater called the Teatro Hidalgo.[25]

Mexico's immediate response to the war also included restricting applications for residency or citizenship in Mexico and assuming the power to examine safety deposit boxes or any other places where money might be concealed.[26] Mexican authorities defended these actions by claiming that under provisions of the Constitution of 1917, the government had the right to take any measures necessary to protect the interests of Mexico.

Throughout its modern history, Mexico had welcomed immigrants from other lands. Until the nineteenth century, the greatest number arrived from Spain, bringing with them the culture and language of their homeland. By the last quarter of the nineteenth century, most immigrants arrived from other countries of Western Europe, although Spaniards in Mexico still outnumbered those from other nations. After Mexico secured its independence from Spain in 1821, the Mexican government encouraged immigration and financial investment in the country. These opportunities helped populate the more isolated areas of Mexico, particularly those where businesses could pursue mining or shipping profitably. Still, the northern Mexican frontier remained sparsely populated. In 1877, as a way to resolve settlement and development problems, Vicente Riva Palacio, Minister of Development, suggested that Mexico could only solve its workforce shortage by promoting immigration.[27] In 1883, President Porfirio Díaz established a law that allowed colonization of national lands. This law provided that settlers could obtain up to 2,500 hectares (6,178 acres) from the government and take ten years to pay for the lands. The incentive was successful and resulted in increased immigration.

Many Italians, Germans, and Japanese arrived during this period. Italy especially encouraged its citizens to emigrate in search of opportunity. Italians went to other European countries, to the United States, to North Africa, and to several Latin American nations. In the early 1880s, Italians began arriving in Mexico at the port of Veracruz. The Mexican government divided the new arrivals into four groups and sent them to different locations for settlement. Groups founded colonies near Huatusco and Tlacolula in Veracruz. A few settled in Michoacán. Some Italians also opted to settle in the Federal District, and at San Vicente in Baja California. Italians who arrived during these years ultimately established six permanent colonies in Mexico.

The Italian colonists faced various difficulties. In Veracruz, the local Mexican press reported that the new arrivals were lazy, unemployed, and reduced to begging on the streets. The newspapers charged that the Mexican government had resettled the immigrants in Veracruz and then abandoned them. Evidently, a few of the Italians with experience as agricultural workers found employment. Some Italians left Mexico for other countries, but those who stayed generally enjoyed good relations with Mexicans. Italians who had settled at Huatusco were moderately successful in agricultural pursuits, as were many who lived in other regions. By 1910 approximately twenty-six hundred Italians lived scattered about in Mexico, principally in the state of Veracruz and in the Federal District.[28]

In 1888, Díaz signed a treaty allowing Japanese immigration to Mexico. Nine years later, the first Japanese colony was established at Escuintla, Chiapas. These were the first Asians to come as a group to settle in Mexico, although some Asians had arrived in Mexico as a consequence of the Acapulco to Manila trade route. A Japanese company bought lands on which to cultivate coffee, tobacco, and caucho (India rubber or gum). By 1910, the colony had approximately fifty-eight settlers working forty hectares (around a hundred acres). Because they could not enter the United States, a number of Japanese immigrants, probably many with relatives north of the border, lived as close as possible to the United States. Several hundred settled in Ciudad Juárez, Mexicali, Ensenada, and Tampico. Others resided in Guadalajara and the Federal District. Those who remained on the coasts were generally fishermen; those who moved inland sometimes worked in mining, although reluctantly. Japanese immigrants also worked in agriculture and occasionally opened small businesses.

Japanese immigrants to Mexico faced many of the same challenges as the Italians and other immigrants, but perhaps because of sharper ethnic, linguistic, and religious differences, the Japanese assimilated less easily than Italians or Germans. Between 1890 and 1949, approximately thirty-five hundred Japanese immigrated legally to Mexico. Many more came but did not have, or seek, legal status.[29] In the early twentieth century, as many as ten thousand immigrants may have passed through Mexico en route to the United States. In 1907, the United States and Japan agreed informally to stop Japanese immigration to the United States. This agreement undoubtedly prompted many Japanese to use Mexico as a conduit for reaching the United States illegally.

Approximately three-quarters of the Japanese who arrived in Mexico between 1890 and 1940 were male. Generally, men arrived, found work, and then sent for the women in their families. Many Japanese immigrants married into Mexican families and ultimately became Mexican citizens. The majority, however, did not seek citizenship. After 1917, professionals including medical doctors, pharmacists, and veterinarians began to arrive. The Japanese living in Mexico earned a reputation as honest, hardworking, and peace-loving. Between 1920 and 1930, many prospered and consolidated their business and property holdings, but, as noted, few became naturalized citizens. Between 1920 and 1940, only 401 Japanese immigrants became Mexican citizens. More might have pursued citizenship, but many encountered bureaucratic obstacles when attempting to have citizenship applications processed. When Mexico broke diplomatic relations with Japan on December 8, 1941, the Japanese community in Mexico suddenly became more visible than most of them wished. They were soon ordered to relocate to specific locations in the country's interior, and their travel was restricted. Some were held in a concentration camp at Temixco, Morelos. The government allowed them only eight days to dispose of their property and relocate.

Germans also immigrated to Mexico before and during the rule of Porfirio Díaz. For instance, in 1867, a group of Germans who had lived in Texas during the United States Civil War left Texas and settled in Tuxpan, Veracruz. By the end of 1868, Germans lived in Manzanillo, in Guadalajara, and near Acapulco. By 1900, approximately five hundred had also settled in Chiapas. During the 1880s, German firms exported various raw materials from Mexico, establishing a significant commercial presence in the country. By the end of the nineteenth century these firms owned most of Mexico's breweries, dominated the electricity-producing companies, and were establishing themselves in banking. After 1900, especially, they became the largest importers of hardware goods and pharmaceuticals in Mexico. By 1910, there were 3,827 documented Germans in Mexico, perhaps as many as 2,500 of whom were citizens. One-third of all Germans in the country lived in the Federal District.[30]

When Germany and Japan invaded other countries at the onset of World War II, threatening the global balance of power, Mexicans believed their government should use all the resources at its disposal to track individuals of Japanese, German, or Italian descent, whether they were citizens or not. By this time, however, agents of the Departamento Confidencial already had people from these countries under surveillance. Mexican officials believed a potential

Axis sabotage of the petroleum industry constituted the major threat to their country. Alfredo Arriola Molina suggested that Japanese property be seized and that people of Japanese descent be required to carry identification cards. He also suggested they be required to report daily to immigration authorities and obtain special permission to travel about the country.[31] Other Mexicans demanded more radical measures. One resident of Jalisco accused the Japanese in the state of nefarious activity. He believed that one Japanese settler, who claimed to be only a poor flower farmer, was, in fact, educated and cultured and probably conducting a secret mission in Mexico. This Mexican also said he feared a Japanese invasion of Mexico's west coast and recommended that Japanese settlers be moved to some interior city where they could be controlled by units of the Mexican Army. In short, he wanted them interned.[32] Their foremost offense, according to him, was their Japanese ancestry. Another Mexican who worked in the government-run petroleum industry in Veracruz reported that he was concerned about two Japanese coworkers. He believed that these individuals presented a danger to the petroleum industry and should be placed in a concentration camp. He neither mentioned nor seemed to care whether these Japanese were Mexican citizens.[33]

The United States often informed Mexico about the activities of Axis-related individuals, especially the Japanese, whom the North Americans considered dangerous. For example, early in the war, the United States authorities alerted Mexican officials that Arturo Yanagihara of San Marcos, Sinaloa, was a dangerous leader of pro-Japanese organizations in that region.[34]

Mexico had not yet relocated any Japanese, German, or Italian immigrants, nor had they forced them into internment camps. However, Mexican officials voiced rising concern about the loyalties of these immigrant communities. Jesús E. Dueñas, the General Secretary of the National Miners Syndicate (Sindicato Nacional de Mineros) at Cananea, Sonora, asked that all workers of Axis heritage be removed from the mines and sent to Mexico City.[35] Leaders of the Leona Vicario Women's League (Liga Femenil Leona Vicario) in Sinaloa advised Avila Camacho that strong action should be taken against the Nazi-fascist groups, meaning all people of Axis descent. They felt this action should include the immediate closing of all Axis consulates throughout Mexico because, they claimed, individuals in these offices were abusing the laws of the country and operating centers of espionage.[36] As the Departamento Confidencial discovered in Mexico City, they were not far wrong.

Soon after the government began to relocate the Japanese in Mexico, some Mexicans in the frontier wanted even more drastic measures taken against people with Axis connections who lived among them. Jorge Gálvez, the president of the local civil defense committee at Yaqui, Sonora, wanted to know why the German, Italian, and Japanese settlers residing in the Yaqui Valley had not been forced to move to Mexico City, especially in view of the pro-Nazi propaganda that continued to circulate in the region. Gálvez wanted the valley cleared of Axis supporters because of the region's agricultural importance.[37] According to Gálvez, many Axis-aligned individuals had been sent to Mexico City during 1942, but a few were slowly returning to the frontier. He did not think this should be allowed as long as the war continued. He also was not certain those returning had official permission to do so. Many Mexicans living in the frontier and various other areas of the country shared Gálvez's concern, and they regularly informed the government about the activities of suspected Axis sympathizers.[38]

Although the Mexican government systematically relocated individuals with Axis ties to the interior, Mexicans throughout the country called for even stronger government action. Petroleum workers in Veracruz demanded restrictions on German and Japanese workers at the Minatitlán Refinery (La Refinería de Minatitlán) in Veracruz. One Mexican worker reported that Carlos J. Ziegler, a man of German descent married to a Mexican woman, represented an obvious example of the threat of sabotage lurking at the refinery and suggested Ziegler be interned somewhere in the interior.[39] Through the work of the agents of the Departamento Confidencial and other agencies, the government steadily intensified its monitoring of Axis-related individuals and any others considered to be a threat to Mexico.[40] The role of the Secretariat of the Treasury and Public Credit (Secretaría de Hacienda y Crédito Público) was especially critical in monitoring threats, as this agency had the power to control all financial and business assets of foreign companies and investors.[41]

Agents of the Departamento Confidencial followed leads about possible subversion, investigating hundreds of tips from Mexicans who claimed they knew of subversive activities.[42] Some of these claims were obviously exaggerated or completely false. For example, one rumor held that a journalist from the United States had heard that Hideki Tojo, Japanese wartime prime minister, had traveled to Baja California before the war to organize the Japanese community there as part of a fifth column.[43] In another incident, an agent of the Departamento Confidencial reported that one of his sources told him an Italian was seen about a hundred kilometers from San Luis Potosí carrying a shortwave radio and a machine gun.[44]

After December 7, 1941, these reports became more frequent and more detailed. For instance, according to another source, Carlos Retelsdorf, born in Mexico of German parents and married to a Mexican woman, had a shortwave radio transmitter and had been heard talking on it in German at three o'clock in the morning. The person who offered this report suspected that Retelsdorf was a spy.[45] A Mexican naval officer stationed near Acapulco reported that the Japanese in his area were in contact with other Axis sympathizers via shortwave radio transmissions. He also believed that a Japanese businessman, Federico Ashida, who owned an electrical generating plant nearby, could not be trusted to remain loyal to Mexico.[46] Another Mexican claimed that Rafael Oseki and Eduardo Taquiuchi, who owned a rayon factory in Chiapas, were Axis sympathizers and cooperated with the local Nazis. This source suggested that the government at least place these two Japanese under constant surveillance, if not in a concentration camp. Other Mexicans in Chiapas suggested that all people of German, Japanese, and Italian descent be placed in concentration camps.[47] One Mexican claimed that petroleum worker George Adamik, a German employee, was a member of the Nazi fifth column and had caused trouble at a government petroleum facility near Veracruz. The government, insisted the source, should expel this man from Mexico.[48] Finally, another Mexican suggested that there was fifth column agitation in Mexican factories that made arms and ammunition, as well as among railroad construction crews.[49] These complaints and reports of the presence and activities of Axis sympathizers were numerous and often more speculative than factual. (Departamento Confidencial agents frequently reported this type of information, but no follow-up information is included in the files.)

Some Germans found themselves facing charges of subversion as late as April 1945. For example, agents of the Departamento Confidencial had carefully investigated the activities of Federico Nolde, a German citizen, during the war. Late in 1943, Carmen T. Wilson, a Mexican citizen by birth, informed the government that Nolde had made a business deal with her husband concerning property in Oaxaca. Nolde refused to pay the $15,000 he owed, claiming the figure had been miscalculated. He apparently owned ranch lands and other businesses in Oaxaca and Veracruz and traveled between the two states frequently. The Wilsons proceeded to file a lawsuit against Nolde and to notify the Secretary of Gobernación of the dispute, hoping to force Nolde to pay his debt. Once it became clear that he would not, the Wilsons decided to create problems for Nolde. Wilson accused him of being a rabid Nazi who was trying to propagandize agricultural workers in both states to support Germany in the war.

The chief of the Departamento Confidencial ordered an investigation into these charges.[50] Apparently, Nolde had once been involved in some questionable financial deals over ranch property, perhaps with the Wilsons. The agents also heard, but could not verify, that Nolde was a strong supporter of Germany and, possibly, a Gestapo agent. Eduardo Miguel Wilson Rey, Carmen's husband, also gave a deposition to the Departamento Confidencial about Nolde. The accused, however, claimed the Wilsons were after his property and businesses in Oaxaca and Veracruz. They were hoping to get the government to incarcerate him in Perote with other political prisoners. Supporters and detractors of the Wilsons gave formal depositions. Nolde insisted that one of the so-called witnesses to his agreement with the Wilsons, Juan Cayetano, was a bootlegger who was drunk most of the time.[51] Nolde's supporters insisted that the only connections Nolde had with his homeland were a small pension for his World War I service and some relatives who still lived there.

Once the investigation was under way, Nolde was ordered to Mexico City. He resided there until the end of May, when Gobernación permitted him to return to Oaxaca. As far as the government was concerned, at this time there was no way to determine whether Nolde was guilty of anything other than being German. In July 1946, Carmen Wilson asked Gobernación to continue the investigation. Apparently, however, the Mexican government was finished with the affair, as nothing further surfaced about this litigation. By 1949, Nolde was living in Puebla, where he sought to renew his passport in order to return to Germany. He said he wanted to return to help rebuild Germany, but he also complained that he had faced continuing difficulties in Mexico. He had bought a small ranch in Puebla only to learn that local political leaders remained hostile after the war, refusing to pay him for products he had sold them.[52]

As the war progressed, the Mexican government augmented its initial strategy of relocation and internment with other precautionary measures designed to limit Axis activity in Mexico. In January 1942, Mexican authorities suspended their practice of granting letters of naturalization to citizens of Germany, Japan, and Italy. In addition, the government revoked the citizenship of any person from these countries who had been naturalized after January 1, 1939. By the end of that month, the government had extended this law to encompass those who were originally citizens of Bulgaria, Hungary, and Romania. The Mexican congress also granted the president extraordinary powers to act against any Axis groups in the country. Mexico declared that its actions were necessary for the protection of Pan American security.[53]

Mexican authorities especially feared sabotage on the west coast of Mexico and along the US border. Many Mexicans believed that the Japanese on the coast were particularly dangerous. In late 1941 and early 1942, in order to protect the coasts from Japanese invasion, the government had advised Japanese living in coastal areas that they must relocate to the interior of the country. Those in Baja California were instructed to go to Mexico City or Guadalajara, where they were required to register so that agents of Gobernación could monitor their movements.[54] Mexican officials believed that Japanese fishermen who worked off Baja California and into the Gulf of California should not be allowed to repatriate to Japan, either, because they knew the coasts too well and might help the Japanese plan an invasion of Mexico. Some of the Japanese recognized the position they were in and wanted to repatriate to Japan. Fifty-eight people actually applied to do so, and a few were allowed to leave by late 1942.[55] (During 1941 and 1942 the government participated in exchanges of Japanese in Mexico who wished to return home and Mexicans caught in Japan when war began.[56])

About two thousand Japanese lived in Baja California. A week after informing the Japanese on the west coast that they should relocate to the interior, the government became more adamant. The Secretario de Gobernación Alemán Valdés ordered officials to round up any Japanese who remained in Mexicali. From there, the net expanded to include surrounding areas. By

January 15, the Mexicali Japanese were all in Mexico City. Approximately 370 Japanese adults and 328 children, including those who had left before the roundup, had registered with local authorities in preparation for relocation. Most Japanese near Mexicali were farmers, and the government decided that they could maintain their businesses and property, but for the duration of the war they were required to turn over administration of these assets to Mexican nationals.[57] Some of those who left the region liquidated their property, fearing that they would lose it anyway.[58] A few Japanese tried to protect themselves from coercive relocation by employing Mexican attorneys to petition the government on their behalf. Through their attorneys, these Japanese agricultural workers stated that they had lived in Mexico for fifteen to thirty years, had all tried to become naturalized citizens but had not succeeded, and all remained loyal to Mexico. The government was unresponsive to these arguments.[59]

Agents of the Departamento Confidencial played a role in these relocations. Records indicate that Agent Antonio de P. Araujo investigated Mitori Shiyama, who had lived for many years with his family in the port city of Coatzacoalcos, Veracruz. The agent reported that Shiyama was the head of the Japanese community in the city, adding that three years earlier, when a Japanese warship visited the port, the ship's captain had invited Shiyama and his wife to join him for dinner on board the vessel. The captain had seated Shiyama immediately to his right for dinner, a gesture the agent considered ominous. The agent also believed that a Japanese photographer who had been present at the dinner should be relocated.[60] The government assigned all these Japanese to Mexico City but allowed them to travel back and forth several times to complete business transactions.

The investigation by agent Antonio de P. Araujo into the activities of Enrique F. Kohashi, a naturalized Mexican citizen, was typical of the treatment endured by the Japanese during the war. The local army commander in Ciudad Ixtepec, Oaxaca, first detained Kohashi and then sent him, accompanied by a military escort, to agent Araujo for questioning. Araujo learned that Kohashi owned several coffee plantations in Tapachula, Chiapas, but lived in Ciudad Ixtepec some of the time. Araujo tried to interview Kohashi, but he refused to cooperate. General Gómez Velasco told the agent that Kohashi was a dangerous individual: a very wealthy Japanese who owned a shortwave radio. He claimed Kohashi had placed cash, amounting to more than $205,000 pesos, in local banks, but shortly before the investigation the funds had suddenly and mysteriously disappeared. Gómez Velasco suggested that Kohashi had withdrawn and hidden the funds to keep the Mexican government from confiscating or freezing them. Kohashi had eight children, one of whom lived and worked in Mexico City and also owned several coffee farms. This son was also apparently wealthy and lived in a palatial estate with gardens and a magnificent library. In his report, Araujo alleged that the businesses run by this family provided a front for subversive Japanese activities in Mexico. Another Kohashi son who lived in Veracruz worked in the petroleum industry in Minatitlán. He also had three shortwave radios in his house, and Araujo considered him a dangerous threat to the petroleum industry. The existence of the radios—and the fact that the father was wealthy and traveled back and forth between Oaxaca, Chiapas, and Veracruz—were sufficient evidence of subversion for Araujo, who informed his chief of his intent to send the father and the son from Veracruz to Mexico City for internment. He also sent a German, Mathias Shiller, with the group. Army Capitán Pablo Cabrera escorted the men to Mexico City. On July 28, 1942, the three men were turned over to the Departamento Confidencial for questioning and observation. Kohashi and his son were allowed to live in Mexico City but were required to report frequently to the government to prove they were still complying with residence rules.[61]

Once agent Araujo had ordered Kohashi and his son to Mexico City, he resumed his investigations into Axis activities in Oaxaca. The deeper he delved into these matters, the more clandestine operations he claimed to have discovered. He became convinced that the Japanese government had been establishing and operating an intelligence-gathering system in Veracruz, Oaxaca, and surrounding regions before the attack on Pearl Harbor. He claimed that Japan had systematically accredited many more diplomatic agents than necessary. Additionally, he believed many Japanese had come to the region under false pretenses, claiming intentions to work in agriculture, commerce, and industry.

In fact, Araujo had even been able to tie Kohashi to these activities, and the agent reported that he had conclusively identified Kohashi, still interned in Mexico City, as the recipient of a large sum of money to be used after the Japanese captured Pearl Harbor. Araujo alleged that Kohashi had been instructed to rent a ship large enough to carry Japanese troops from Hawaii to Veracruz, where the Japanese would capture the petroleum fields as their first step in invading Mexico. This, he suggested, explained all of Kohashi's trips to Veracruz. Araujo even claimed that Kohashi was the principal spy for the Japanese as Japan prepared for this invasion. Araujo also accused women in Kohashi's family of spying, alleging that Kohashi's wife and daughter-in-law were assisting their husbands in espionage while the men were detained in Mexico City.

Araujo concluded his report with rumors of further Japanese plans to bring aircraft and other war materials to the Veracruz region.[62] Araujo had gleaned much of his information from his conversations with General Gómez Velasco, who based his knowledge entirely upon hearsay. In fact, there was no evidence that any of his information about the Kohashi family was accurate. They were probably guilty only of being wealthy foreigners who were ethnically and socially different from the majority population.

During this period, the Departamento Confidencial also investigated Dr. Toshio Shimizu, a medical doctor who had lived in Mazatlán since 1912 and was a naturalized Mexican citizen. Evidently, Shimizu had made a great deal of money performing abortions and had invested his money in mining and other businesses. In the process, he had made enemies, but he also had carefully cultivated support among local government officials. When the relocation of Axis nationals began in 1942, Shimizu was sent under guard to Mexico City. At that time he requested permission to return to Mazatlán. Municipal authorities and many private citizens in Mazatlán supported his request. Evidently, Shimizu had been generous to the city, funding the construction of parks and gardens and participating in local activities to promote the growth and development of the region. The governor of the state of Sinaloa, Coronel Rodolfo T. Loaiza, assured Gobernación that Shimizu constituted no threat to Mexico. The governor also wrote to Gobernación that this Japanese was an outstanding citizen and should be allowed to return permanently to Sinaloa. In turn, the governor promised that he would monitor all Japanese activities in the region. There were others, however, who insisted that Shimizu was not a "desirable" citizen. One of these dissenters claimed that Shimizu had aborted children, and in many cases women had died as a consequence. Some also questioned his loyalty, and it was rumored that he was an officer in the Japanese military. Again, there was no evidence that Shimizu had taken any steps to support Japanese militarism, but he had evidently performed abortions, which rankled many Mexicans. Early in 1943, Shimizu received permission from Gobernación to return to Mazatlán permanently.[63] Once again, the removal or reinstatement of a person of Axis descent depended upon wealth and influence.

Despite the efforts of pro-Japanese groups either to lessen restrictions or terminate the concentration policy, Mexico did not end the program until January 2, 1945. During the war, the government used funds from seized Japanese assets to provide small incomes for the interned Japanese.[64] Although fewer Germans had suffered wartime internment, by the end of the war the Mexican government was putting frozen German funds to similar use. Mexico kept what appeared to be careful records about who received funds and how much each person received.[65] By August 1945, approximately four thousand Japanese had been interned in Guadalajara, Mexico City, and other locations.[66] The number of Germans was much smaller, and few of them suffered internment to the extent of the Japanese.

Although many Mexican government officials did not consider Italians a serious threat, agents of the Departamento Confidencial sometimes investigated them. The subject of one investiation was Antonio Busterna Gagliani, an Italian national with legal residency in Mexico. Gagliani was married to a Mexican and usually resided in Mexicali or Tijuana. When Gobernación began to relocate Axis-related individuals from the west coast to the interior, Busterna Gagliani began a writing campaign requesting permission to remain in Baja California. He said he was the manager of a restaurant in Tijuana and claimed he obeyed all laws and dedicated himself to taking care of his many chickens. He insisted that this poultry business demanded his complete attention, for the birds needed to be vaccinated and their pens cleaned. He insisted he could not be removed to Mexico City—he would lose his restaurant business, and his seven employees would be unemployed and in the street.[67] The Departamento Confidencial conducted a superficial investigation of his past activities, and an agent concluded that the subject was dedicated to his work, had no record of political involvement, and should be allowed to remain in Baja California.[68] Additionally, the chairman of the local committee of hotel workers had written a letter to Miguel Alemán Valdés, explaining that Busterna Gagliani was a model citizen, hardworking, and honest. Several officials of the Territory of Baja California had cosigned the note.[69] On November 3, 1942, the Chief of the Departamento Confidencial, Lelo de Larrea, informed his agents in Tijuana that Busterna Gagliani had received permission from Gobernación to remain in Tijuana for sixty days.[70]

A few days after the government had granted this permission, Col. Rodolfo Sánchez Taboada, Governor of the Territory of Baja California, advised Gobernación that Busterna Gagliani should not be allowed to stay in Baja California. The colonel had investigated the subject, who frequently used an alias, and learned that he was an opium addict. He also had a police record in California, where authorities had jailed him for selling drugs. In fact, he had been jailed six times between 1935 and 1939. He managed to elude a sentence on the first five of these charges, owing to incomplete evidence. On the last charge, however, the courts convicted him and sentenced him to two five-year prison terms for receiving, selling, transporting, and importing opium into California. The judge had suspended the sentences as long as Busterna Gagliani agreed to leave the United States immediately and not return. The Italian had followed these rules until August 1942, when, while driving his Cadillac near San Isidro, California, he was again arrested carrying five grams of opium in the car. How he had escaped to return to Mexico is not indicated in the files. Colonel Sánchez Taboada admitted he could not keep track of this man, and he should immediately be moved to Mexico City.[71]

Further investigation by the Departamento Confidencial made it clear that Busterna Gagliani did not own a restaurant as he claimed. The Secretary of Gobernación promptly cancelled his permission to remain in Tijuana and ordered him to report immediately to Mexico City. Busterna Gagliani complied with the order, but once in the capital he initiated another writing campaign to return to Baja California. From January to May, he also claimed he had to return to take care of his wife, but Gobernación refused this request. Busterna Gagliani enjoyed the support of several workers' organizations in Baja California, however, and the leaders of these groups wrote directly to Miguel Alemán Valdés, Secretary of Gobernación. Early in June, Busterna Gagliani was able to secure permission directly from Alemán Valdés to return to the peninsula for ninety days.[72] There was no further correspondence about this individual. He must have had money and influence at his disposal, for he evidently remained in Tijuana for the duration of the war, well beyond his ninety-day limit.

Mexican officials frequently issued special permissions for Axis-related individuals to remain in or return to their place of residence. In most instances, this happened for no apparent reason. One might surmise, however, that those allowed to return to their resident states were wealthy and could afford to bribe officials for this opportunity. Alemán Valdés and his staff were notorious for accepting financial favors from businesses and individuals. Mexican military zone commanders regularly complained to Gobernación that too often the army helped remove Axis individuals to Mexico City, or some other interior location, only to learn that they did not remain there for long. General Francisco L. Urquizo advised Alemán Valdés that this was a serious problem because those individuals often involved themselves in pro-Axis propaganda efforts. Urquizo also accused these individuals of watching ship traffic in the ports in order to keep the German government informed of military activities. One such individual was José Cantisani Peluso, of Italian heritage, who was allowed to return to Veracruz for thirty days to finish some personal business. Cantisani Peluso remained for several months, however, and traveled all along the coast, apparently ignoring his deadline. No evidence surfaced that this Italian had gathered or sent military intelligence to German, Italian, or Japanese agents, but the Mexican Army opposed making exceptions for a few important and wealthy individuals. The fact that military commanders on both coasts complained about such disparities suggests this practice was widespread. In all of these scenarios, the individual granted an exception was a businessman with considerable financial assets. All were financially capable of negotiating with high-ranking Mexican officials for their freedom of movement.[73]

Occasionally, foreign-born individuals, Germans especially, contacted President Manuel Avila Camacho's office directly, but even in such instances the letters of complaint were merely forwarded to Gobernación and then to the Departamento Confidencial for action. Werner Barke, who had been interned at the Casa de Detención (Detention Quarters) at Tlacopac in Mexico City, lodged typical complaints about the agents. Although he did not specify what type of agents these were, they were likely those of the Departamento Confidencial. Barke told the president that two operatives, brothers Manuel and Alvarito González, had arrived at his residence in Villa Obregón, Distrito Federal, and taken him to jail at the Santa Julia station. The next day, the agents returned to his house and absconded with many of his possessions, including six meters of English gabardine cloth, one pair of initialed gold cufflinks, thirty fine silk ties, four new pair of monogrammed pajamas, various paintings, a new Jantzen suit, and many other items. Barke insisted to Avila Camacho that these actions constituted mistreatment of political prisoners.[74]

The Departamento Confidencial was involved in another investigation that might have been justified but was not conducted professionally. Agents discovered that Guillermo Schuppenhausen was born in Germany, but left for Spain in 1911 to learn Spanish. In March 1912, he returned to Germany briefly, was called for military service, but failed the army physical examination. Almost immediately, he left for Mexico, arriving late that year. He went to work for a company representing the House of Krupp, a German industrial firm. Schuppenhausen later worked for other German companies in Mexico, mostly as an accountant, and at one of these firms he eventually became a partner. In 1917, he joined the local German Club (El Casino Alemán), paying his dues faithfully until the organization closed during the war. He was also one of the organizers of the German Charity Society (Sociedad de Beneficencia Alemana). He married a Mexican woman, Marta Alemán, in 1926, establishing local ties. He traveled back to Germany for the first time in 1923 and returned with his wife in 1929, 1935, and again in 1938. When he saw that Germany was preparing for war, however, he quickly returned to Mexico. In 1940, Schuppenhausen asked the Mexican government to grant him citizenship, and he became a naturalized Mexican citizen on July 9, 1940. He would soon find, however, that his citizenship was of little value in protecting him from treatment as a Nazi sympathizer.

Mexican agents who infiltrated German companies and social organizations compiled a file on Schuppenhausen. These agents noted that the Germans they investigated typically spoke German among themselves and Spanish when they were around Mexicans, raising suspicion. When Mexico entered the war against the Axis powers, the government made it impossible for individuals like Schuppenhausen to continue working. In 1943, Gobernación ordered his company to terminate his employment. For the rest of the war, he relied upon his wife's family for financial survival. After the war, he petitioned the Mexican government to allow him to return to work, but it was well into 1946 before he was allowed to do so. Investigative agencies could prove nothing disloyal about this German's activities before or during the war, and it is doubtful that he had any ties to the Nazis.[75]

The Departamento Confidencial investigated other Germans who in all likelihood would have avoided any contact whatsoever with the Nazi regime. Among those who suffered at the hands of the agency were two Jews, Federico Blumenthal Schwab and his wife, Matilda. Mr. Blumenthal Schwab worked as a sales agent for several companies, including the Amer-Trade company, the Puegil Bros., and Santa Claus de México. In January 1939, he and his wife had arrived at Veracruz, Mexico, as refugees and lived in Cuernavaca until they were summoned to appear in Mexico City. On January 6, 1944, the couple appeared in Mexico City for questioning by agents of the Departamento Confidencial. He told the agents that he was born in 1898 in Wiesbaden, Germany, and had been a German citizen until the Nazi regime deprived him of that status. The reason he had come to Mexico was that during 1938 he had been interned in a concentration camp near Königsberg, Germany. Somehow he had arranged to escape from the camp, but he had to agree to leave Germany. He and his wife traveled from Hamburg to the United States, where they remained briefly, and then moved on to Veracruz. (At that time, the United States was not admitting German Jews seeking asylum from the Hitler regime.) Blumenthal Schwab claimed that Nazi police had confiscated his funds and all of his possessions, including his passport. He had, however, found financial success in Mexico, earning approximately a thousand pesos monthly as a commercial agent for companies based in the United States and Argentina. He informed the agents that he had served in the German Army from 1914 to 1918, rising to the rank of first lieutenant. He said he had never belonged to any political party and that in Mexico his affiliations were with Jewish organizations and support groups. He spoke German, English, French, and Spanish. His wife and her son from an earlier marriage spoke all of these languages as well.

With this investigation complete, the chief of the Departamento Confidencial recorded that he saw no indication these individuals were dangerous and that he believed they were who they said they were. This type of investigation illustrates the fears of Mexican authorities that some Nazi agents might have posed as displaced Jews to enter Mexico. Thus disguised, such agents could have sent information back to Germany through the Gestapo or some other Nazi organization.[76]

On the other hand, considerable evidence exists that Mexico did not always vigorously pursue those who were suspected of Nazi activities. Herman Dorner, born of German parents in Uruguay, was married to the sister of a high Nazi official and lived in Mexico on a business visa. Dorner was so well connected with German diplomats in the city that he was constantly attending embassy and private parties with Hitler's diplomatic corps. University educated in Uruguay, Dorner spoke Spanish, Portuguese, French, and German. He was from an extremely wealthy and influential family with business interests in several European countries and throughout South America. Beginning in July 1942, agents of the Departamento Confidencial kept Dorner and his wife under constant surveillance, and Herman Dorner was interned in Perote. One agent, after monitoring the Dorners' telephone during Dorner's internment, reported that an individual called their residence to advise Mrs. Dorner that things would be less difficult for them after her husband talked with General Maximino Avila Camacho, the president's brother. He claimed to be only joking, but offered to help the couple.[77] During early April 1943 Dorner's wife got permission to visit him in Perote by telling Mexican authorities that she needed to take him money to buy necessities. Two weeks after she made the trip, Dorner was allowed to return to Mexico City.

Another influential Nazi was Ernst Hopf, who was considered to be one of the most active and dangerous German agents in Mexico. Apparently, however, he initially escaped any serious repercussions for his espionage activities in Mexico. When Mexico decided to crack down on Nazis and Nazi sympathizers, Hopf was imprisoned for a short time at Perote, then allowed to move to Mexico City. He was placed under house arrest, under which conditions prisoners were allowed telephones and visitors and, seemingly, were not further molested. It quickly became known to officials of Gobernación that Hopf was a friend of the Chief of the Department of Immigration. According to one source in Mexico, Hopf and other Germans had bought their way out of Perote. The only ones who remained incarcerated were those who were not wealthy enough to purchase their freedom.[78]

One German in Mexico City with sufficient resources to win immunity from restrictions was Dr. Friedrich Pfeiffer, who, along with his wife, Amalia, had become a naturalized citizen. Agents and police investigators charged the couple with being committed Nazis who distributed pro-Nazi propaganda in the city. Nonetheless, on August 6, 1942, the Pfeiffers received permission to travel to their Cuernavaca home. No doubt under the instruction of a superior, Lelo de Larrea, as director of the Departamento Confidencial, issued a "to whom it may concern" informing his agents of this special permission.[79] Similar permissions were granted to Pfeiffer throughout the next several months, despite continuing warnings from agents that he was engaging in pro-Nazi activities.[80] Although there is no extant evidence revealing who was behind the granting of special privileges to wealthy Axis sympathizers, it was no doubt some high-ranking person in Gobernación, or perhaps Secretary Alemán Valdés himself, who was notoriously corrupt.

In addition to its surveillance of normally nonpolitical Germans, Japanese, and Italians living throughout Mexico, the Departamento Confidencial concentrated considerable effort on monitoring the members of the Spanish Falange. The Falange, founded in Spain in 1933 by José Primo de Rivera, the son of Miguel Primo de Rivera, was a right-wing political organization that had supported the revolt of General Francisco Franco against the Republican government of Spain. It was strongly antiliberal and anti-Communist. The Falange represented landowners, business people, students, and middle class Catholics. By the time of the Spanish Civil War, the Falange publically supported the Nazi government in Germany.

In 1936, Spanish Falangists began organizing in Mexico. Agusto Ibáñez Serrano, a leader in the Casa de España in Mexico, along with the Spanish minister of foreign relations, nominally directed Falange activities in Mexico, although Georg Nicolaus, Gestapo chief, may have made the final decisions. Perhaps not all of the Falangists were Nazi sympathizers, but evidence suggests many were. Falange supporters were located primarily in the country's northern frontier, near the United States–Mexican border, and in Puebla, although they were present in all sections of the country. In the late 1930s, some native Mexicans became disillusioned with the direction of the Revolution and turned to the Falange, which at that time was increasing its propaganda and organizational activities in Mexico. Falange supporters included wealthy members of the Spanish colony who held vital financial interests in domestic mercantile pursuits, the publishing sector, and the processed food industry. This group had no sympathy for the liberalism of the Cárdenas regime. The organization was well-financed, receiving money from Spain and donations from the Spanish community within Mexico.[81] While the most intense effort to monitor the Falange was focused in Mexico City, agents were also sent to strategic areas such as the port at Veracruz.

Mexican agents learned that Ibáñez Serrano, a representative of the Franco government in Mexico, posed as the director of a financial investment company and most likely operated a cover enterprise to fund the Mexican Falange movement. The group in Mexico comprised two parallel organizations, one official and operating in sight of Mexican authorities and the other clandestine. Ibáñez Serrano operated the official branch, while Eulogio Celorio Sordo led the clandestine operation. Both men were Spaniards. Sordo arrived in Mexico during the first week of July 1941 to provide more aggressive leadership. José Enrique Carrillo and José Huerta, also Spaniards and veterans of the Spanish Civil War, were the commanders of Falange militia forces in Mexico. The Falange held meetings in cafes, public parks, gardens, or other places where they would be inconspicuous.[82] The organization was carefully organized with officers and troops organized in a hierarchy similar to that of a military system.[83] According to agents of the Departamento Confidencial, some of the groups supported internal discord, advocated passive resistance to the government, and planned sabotage activities.[84] Agents were under orders at all times to learn the names of all Falange members, and they devoted considerable time to this task.[85] When Pedro Amieva Noceda, a Spaniard, arrived in Mexico, agents immediately investigated his background. They learned that he was an experienced Falange member who during the Spanish Civil War had infiltrated Republican organizations and supplied information to the Franco forces. His information had resulted in the death of several Republican supporters. Almost as soon as he arrived in Mexico, agents of the Departamento Confidencial monitored his activities twenty-four hours a day.[86] They were, however, unable to catch him violating any Mexican laws. He remained free to move about the country.

In July of 1943, the Departamento Confidencial dispatched more agents to continue watching the various Falange organizations throughout the country. At least one of these operatives was a female, Antonia Elsa Martínez, who was assigned to monitor women's groups. All agents were to report personally to Chief Lelo de Larrea Domínguez as quickly as they completed their work.[87] Ten days later, agents reported that they had heard pro-Franco talk among Falangists and that each of their meeting places prominently featured a picture of Franco. The agents heard nothing specific about their activities, because any serious planning was done in small executive groups where the agents could not monitor what was said. The agents also learned that the leadership of the Sinarquista movement, officially a subsidiary of the Falange, worked constantly with Falange leaders to promote the two organizations in Mexico.[88] In fact, agents were able to confirm ties between the two organizations, for leaders of the Sinarquistas met on a regular basis with the Falange. Because of its pro-Nazi stance, the Sinarquistas had been under surveillance for some time, and Avila Camacho eventually outlawed the group in 1944. According to Departamento agents there was an organization directed by four Mexicans—the Hispanic Council (Consejo de Hispanidad) in Mexico City—that served to tie all pro-Axis and pro-Franco groups together.[89] Investigations into the activities of the Falange continued throughout the war, but after 1943, when it became obvious that the Axis would not win the war, the Falange was perceived as less of a threat.

By 1944 the agents had broadened their investigations to include Spanish priests serving at several locations in the country who were perhaps involved in Falange activity. The agents compiled detailed records of the activities of these clerics, and one agent remarked that "all of these priests were active propagandists for the Falange, and they were trying to foment trouble within reactionary groups in Mexico."[90]

The activities of the Departamento Confidencial during World War II focused primarily on foreigners or their organizations that might threaten Mexican security. By 1940, upon the ascendancy of Manuel Avila Camacho to the presidency, lingering threats from old revolutionaries had diminished. Mexico still suffered decentralization tendencies, but political party organization that tied regional strongmen to Mexico City, along with the declining influence of the military in politics, slowly encouraged the establishment of civilian leadership at all levels of government. In 1946, upon Miguel Alemán Valdés's ascendancy to the presidency, Mexico had its first civilian president in decades.

CHAPTER FIVE

CONCLUSION

Since 1821, when Mexico secured its independence from Spain, its governing elites have employed whatever means available to centralize control and retain power. They sometimes eliminated their enemies, but just as often they sought to weaken opposition by creating division among opponents. To accomplish their goals, those in power had to identify factions that threatened either themselves or their regimes. Governments collected this information by assorted means. In Mexico, the army gathered information its high command believed constituted a threat either to the country or to the military. At various times, the government also dispatched special agents to collect information about political and social conditions, to ascertain the validity of rumors, or to determine the seriousness of a particular threat. The elites who controlled the country most often justified this internal espionage as necessary to the protection of the country from foreign intervention or the preservation of order and security. They also viewed internal stability as synonymous with their retention of power. This view justified any action they might take. When government leaders equate national well-being with the self-interests of specific individuals or of a particular group in power, defense of the country ultimately leads to a corruption of the concept of internal security and distorts how nationalism is defined. Mexican leaders have frequently considered consolidation of power as a means of combating regionalism and creating a national political culture. Within the Mexican political and social system, regional caudillismo, or strongman rule, seemingly allowed local power brokers to act above the law. Historically, Mexican presidents have understood the political and social forces at work in Mexico and the danger they sometimes posed for the country. In order to counter the forces deemed most dangerous, and to stifle regionalism, they frequently employed cajoling, bribery, armed force, and myriad other means against regional chieftains.

In the decades following independence from Spain in 1820, Mexico generally suffered regional caudillo rule. During the 1870s until 1910, General

Porfirio Díaz sought to eliminate, persuade, or bribe uncooperative caudi-llos. His success brought new economic advancement and stability to the country. After 1910, and lasting throughout the armed combat stage of the Mexican Revolution, regional caudillismo again became a significant prob-lem in the country. Using methods similar to those Díaz used before him, Carranza sought to gain control of these regional strongmen. El Primer Jefe used methods of all sorts, including the use of special agents to monitor the activities of those who opposed him. He was successful for a short time. Where it was necessary, he recognized regional autonomy as long as the local caudillo did not act against the government.

During the revolutionary period of 1910–1920, most leaders of oppos-ing factions sent spies to infiltrate enemy forces in order to collect military information. Between 1915 and 1920, Carranza, realizing how important information gathering was to his political success, sent agents throughout the country and into his enemies' camps. While Carranza organized espio-nage agencies fairly efficiently, the methods used to collect information were not always reliable. After his death in 1920, national leaders systematically improved these methods, relying increasingly upon internal espionage to monitor potential enemies, real or imagined. These leaders employed several means of gathering information. The most important and long-lasting inter-nal espionage agency was the Dirección General de Investigaciones Políti-cas y Sociales (DGIPS). Under this agency, the Departamento Confidencial conducted investigations within and occasionally outside of Mexico. This department operated independently of other intelligence-gathering opera-tions, such as those of the various Mexican consulates in the United States.

Gaining cooperation from the regional chieftains and suppressing their military impulses remained a problem for presidents Alvaro Obregón, Plu-tarco Elías Calles, and Lázaro Cárdenas. In 1920, upon General Obregón's ascendancy to the presidency, Mexico had no national army. In fact, there were several armies all controlled by local caudillos who had become gen-erals due to their success in raising armies during the revolution. Obregón began the process of institutionalizing and professionalizing the national army by promoting military education and incorporating the armies of the caudillos into a national army. In putting the caudillo's armies on the fed-eral payroll, the president hoped to turn their impulses away from politics and toward military professionalism. His efforts to consolidate the armies under national control led to a military revolt in 1923. Obregón won this first contest, had the rebellious officers shot or exiled, and promoted younger and better-educated professional officers. Despite these measures, military revolts continued to occur until 1938.

General Plutarco Elías Calles, as Secretario de Gobernación in the Obregón administration, recognized the need to monitor military and political movements opposed to the government. In 1922 and 1923, to gather information about the opposition, Calles established the formal framework for the Departamento Confidencial, with the help of his close associate General Joaquín Amaro. Calles lowered military spending, supported military educational programs, and began transferring generals away from their home power bases. Calles crushed two military revolts between 1923 and 1927 and, after becoming president in 1924, controlled the country until General Lázaro Cárdenas assumed the presidency in 1934. Calles surveilled the actions of veteran army generals and monitored suspicious political activities in general, through reports by his supporters in the army and investigations by the Departamento Confidencial. Calles also organized a national political party in order to consolidate his control and intructed its agents to monitor opposition in the army, the Catholic Church, and labor organizations in the country.

During his presidency, Cárdenas used the methods and agencies Calles had established to continue military reforms and monitor political opposition. His reorganization of the national political party, control of regional chieftains, and leadership of the Departamento Confidencial allowed him to pursue programs of consolidation. In 1940, Cárdenas passed on to General Manuel Avila Camacho a much stronger and more fully institutionalized national government. Avila Camacho completed the consolidation of power in the central government through the reorganization of the national political party and the elimination of the army from the political sector that had begun with Calles. Throughout all of these changes, reports of the agents of the Departamento Confidencial exposed opposition to national policies, contributing to the stability of the government, the institutional development of the Mexican political system, and ultimately the centralization of authority.

During the period covered in this study, the Departamento Confidencial was not generally as sinister or efficient as similar internal espionage agencies in Nazi Germany and the USSR. Dissidents and nonconformists frequently disappeared in Germany and the USSR. In Mexico, the elimination of political opponents surely occurred as a consequence of the information the Departamento Confidencial provided, but murdering opponents was not part of the daily operation of the agency. Likewise, in the United States, the FBI employed threats, propaganda, and intimidation to stifle the actions of individuals or groups, but no extant record of elimination has been uncovered, except in instances of criminal violence.

In 1947, with the creation of the Dirección Federal de Seguridad (DFS), the Departamento Confidencial decreased in importance but continued its surveillance of social and political activities. The DFS existed until 1985, when its functions were merged with Dirección de Investigaciones y Seguridad Nacional (DISEN) and other agencies. Between 1920 and 1947, Mexican leadership generally refined and institutionalized the methods of gathering information, controlling social protest, and subverting threats to the country.[1]

The Departamento Confidencial collected thousands of pages of documents, some useful and some not so useful. In their reports, agents frequently offered interpretations of this material intelligence. The interpretations were not always accurate; sometimes they were self-serving, slanted by an agent's personal beliefs or his or her dislike of some individual or group. Mexican leaders were frequently suspicious of opposition and often paranoid to the extent of myopia. During World War II, the Departamento Confidencial shifted its focus toward investigating individuals and businesses with Axis ties. Agents continued monitoring the activities of political dissidents and radicals in the labor movement, as well as other groups, but government efforts were focused specifically upon those individuals they considered to be enemy aliens.

During the postwar era, the agency monitored dissident groups and individuals. In 1968, when university students and others angry at the government gathered at Tlatelolco to protest grievances, agents were in the midst of the protestors. The students and their supporters had chosen an inauspicious time to incite civil disorder, for the Olympics were in Mexico City that year, and the government was completely intolerant of civil disruption. The

Federal District police and army units brutally quelled this outbreak, but not before considerable violence had erupted. In 1971, protesters again reacted to government policies, and a recurrence of the violence of 1968 erupted with the same results. In both instances, protesters were beaten, imprisoned, or killed, or they simply disappeared. Those who never reappeared were presumed to be murder victims of the government. The Departamento Confidencial sent agents to investigate radical activities and to note how authorities dealt with the eruptions. These reports, along with photographs of the violence, became a permanent part of DGIPS records in the Mexican national archives. During the 1990s, investigators attempting to bring charges against those government elites in power at the time examined the DGIPS files to gather information about the culpability of police and government authorities. Included in this effort were unsuccessful attempts to convict Luis Echeverría for his role in suppressing the disturbances while Secretario de Gobernación and, later, president. Those seeking formal charges argued that Echeverría had ordered brutal reprisals; however, the Mexican court system refused to take punitive action against him.

Using various agencies, Mexico has continued internal espionage into the modern era. Governing individuals or groups have insisted that this internal monitoring is necessary to protect the country and its citizens. How much of this justification is political rationalization cannot be ascertained. Other questions remain difficult to answer. For example, did citizens know that the government was monitoring their actions? In some cases in Mexico, groups were aware that agents were among those in attendance at rallies, but either could not identify them or were unable to stop them from working. In most situations, the majority did not know they were being observed. When individuals or groups were aware of these activities, there was little they could do, except provide disinformation that served group or local interests. There were no demonstrations against the government in response to agents working in a particular area or monitoring a group. Newspapers did not carry stories about agents. Internal espionage was not a political issue as far as the public was concerned. Perhaps the most difficult question is whether, in Mexico, internal espionage greatly assisted ruling elites, although Aaron Navarro makes a strong case for the value of the department's influence in shaping national politics.[2] Beyond those instances cited in the text, the results are mixed. Such is the nature of clandestine operations. There is little doubt, however, that spy operations in Mexico informed the ruling class of potential problems and contributed to the evolution of a stronger central government.

NOTES

CHAPTER 1

1   See Will Fowler, *Santa Anna of Mexico* (Lincoln: University of Nebraska Press, 2007). This excellent work is the most important written about Santa Anna, a local caudillo who occupied the presidency several times. Fowler has delved deeply into the background of Santa Anna, and his work in *Santa Anna* is a "deconstructionist" effort that prompts considerable reinterpretation of this important historical figure. He argues that Santa Anna realized that the decentralization tendencies of Mexico at this time precluded anyone leading the country for a long period without considerable repression of the outlying regions and local leaders. Consequently, although nominally president, he left the Federal District and retreated to his lands, leaving the presidency in the hands of others. Fowler argues that the most important things to Santa Anna were the army, his haciendas, and the country. See also Ruth R. Olivera and Liliane Crété, *Life in Mexico Under Santa Anna, 1822–1855* (Norman: University of Oklahoma Press, 1991).

2   For the methods Díaz used to centralize control of the country, see Paul Garner, *Porfirio Díaz: Profiles in Power* (London: Longman, 2001).

3   James A. Sandos, *Rebellion in the Borderlands: Anarchism and the Plan of San Diego, 1904–1923* (Norman: University of Oklahoma Press, 1992), xv; see also Ward S. Albro, *Always a Rebel: Ricardo Flores Magón and the Mexican Revolution* (Fort Worth: Texas Christian University Press, 1992), and Charles H. Harris and Louis R. Sadler, "The Plan of San Diego and the Mexican–United States War Crisis of 1916: A Reexamination," in *The Border and the Revolution: Clandestine Activities of the Mexican Revolution, 1910–1920*, eds. Harris and Sadler (Silver City, NM: High-Lonesome Books, 1988), 71–98. See also Josefina Moguel Flores, introduction to *El Magonismo en Coahuila* (Monterrey, NL: Grafo Print Editores), 2006.

4   See Paul J. Vanderwood, *Disorder and Progress: Bandits, Police, and Mexican Development* (Wilmington, DE: Scholarly Resources, 1992). This outstanding work on social banditry was first published in 1981 by the University of Nebraska Press.

5   Michael M. Smith, "The Mexican Secret Service in the United States, 1910–1920," *The Americas* 59, no. 1 (July 2002): 65–85. See also W. Dirk Raat, *Revoltosos: Mexico's Rebels in the United States, 1903–1923* (College Station: Texas A&M University Press, 1981), 179. Raat's excellent work focuses upon the activities of Mexican rebels in the United States who opposed the Díaz government and subsequent governments until 1923. He includes activities south of the international line along the frontier with the United States.

6   For a thorough interpretive account of the Mexican Revolution, see Alan Knight, *The Mexican Revolution 2 vols.* (Cambridge: Cambridge University Press, 1986); for a different perspective, see John Mason Hart, *Revolutionary Mexico: The Coming and Process of the Mexican Revolution*, 2nd ed. (Berkeley: University of California Press, 1997).

7   For additional information, see Mark Wasserman, *Persistent Oligarchs: Elites and Politics in Chihuahua Mexico, 1910–1940* (Durham, NC: Duke University Press, 1993). See also Michael C. Meyer, *Mexican Rebel: Pascual Orozco and the Mexican Revolution, 1910–1915* (Lincoln: University of Nebraska Press, 1967), and William H. Beezely, *Insurgent Governor: Abraham González of Chihuahua* (Lincoln: University of Nebraska Press, 1973). For information about the frontier during the Porfiriato, see Miguel Tinker-Salas, *In the Shadow of the Eagles: Sonora and the Transformation of the Border during the Porfiriato* (Berkeley: University of California Press, 1977). For specific information about Victoriano Huerta, see Michael C. Meyer, *Huerta: A Political Portrait* (Lincoln: University of Nebraska Press, 1972).

8   Librorio Villalobos Calderón, "Hacia una historia de la Secretaría de Gobernación," *Solo Historia*, Instituto Nacional de Estudios Históricos de la Revolución Mexicana, 2 (abril–junio de 2000): 65–69.

9   "Proyecto para la formación de un cuerpo de agentes especiales de guerra en el ejército constitutionalista," January 17, 1915, doc. 2459, Manuscritos de don Venustiano Carranza: Centro de Estudios de Historia de México, Fundación Cultural de Condumex, México, DF, hereafter cited as VCT.

10 Many examples of information gathering within Mexico and in the United States exist. See, for example, "Informe de la Oficina de Información y Propaganda," August 2, 3, 1915, XXI, docs. 2459, 5149, 5166, Telegramas, VCT. See also Marta Eugenia García Ugarte, "El chisme en corto o el espionaje profesional en Querétaro," *Eslabones: Revista Semestral de Estudios Regionales* 2 (julio/diciembre 1991): 141–153.

11 Francisco José Cervantes, "Ojos sobre el sur: Carranza y los oaxaqueños," *Eslabones: Revista Semestral de Estudios Regionales* 2 (julio/diciembre 1991): 134–140.

12 Marta Eugenia García Ugarte, "El chisme en corto o el espionaje profesional en Querétaro."

13 J. Guilebardo to Venustiano Carranza, November 5, 1915, XXI, doc. 6574, VCT.

14 See "Memorándum," n.d., XXI, doc. 7691, VCT.

15 See tomo 82, exp. 15, foja 1-2, Dirección General de Investigaciones Políticas y Sociales, Archivo General de la Nación, México, DF, hereafter cited as DGIPS.

16 General Joaquín de la Peña, "Resumen de los breves apuntes para la historia del DEPARTAMENTO CONFIDENCIAL," n.d., but probably May 1934, tomo 58, DGIPS.

17 See Friedrich Katz, *The Secret War in Mexico: Europe, the United States, and the Mexican Revolution* (Chicago: University of Chicago Press, 1981). This work is

widely recognized as the most thoughtful and thorough work about how Germany, Britain, and the United States sought to monitor and influence what occurred in Mexico during World War I.

18 See Smith, "Mexican Secret Service"; Smith, "Carancista Propaganda and the Print Media in the United States: An Overview of Institutions," *The Americas* 52, no. 2 (October 1995): 155–174; Smith, "Gringo Propagandist: George F. Weeks and the Mexican Revolution," *Journalism History* 29, no. 2 (Spring 2003): 2–11. For a thorough explanation of how Carranza employed Mexican consular agents in espionage, see Smith, "Andrés García: Venustiano Carranza's Eyes, Ears, and Voice on the Border," *Mexican Studies (Estudios Mexicanos)* 33, no. 2 (Summer 2007): 355–413.

19 See Linda B. Hall, *Alvaro Obregón: Power and Revolution in Mexico, 1911–1920* (College Station: Texas A&M Press, 1981). This work is an excellent treatment of the role of Obregón in the Mexican Revolution.

20 See Douglas Richmond, *Venustiano Carranza's Nationalist Struggle, 1893–1920* (Lincoln: University of Nebraska Press, 1983). This is a thorough explanation of Carranza's contribution to the Mexican Revolution. See also Josefina Moguel Flores, *Venustiano Carranza: Antología* (México, DF: Instituto Nacional de Estudios Históricos de la Revolución Mexicana, 1986), and Moguel Flores, *Venustiano Carranza: Primer Jefe y Presidente* (Saltillo, Coahuila: Secretaría de Gobernación, 1995). For additional information concerning the confrontation between Woodrow Wilson, Villa, and Carranza, see Joseph A. Stout Jr., *Border Conflict: Villistas, Carrancistas, and the Punitive Expedition, 1916–1920* (Fort Worth: Texas Christian University Press, 1999); see also Joseph A. Stout Jr., "La expedición punitiva," *Provincias Internas*, año 11, 7/8 (otoño e invierno 2002–2003): 93–107.

21 See Douglas W. Richmond, ed., *La Frontera Mexico-Estados Unidos Durante la Época Revolucionaria, 1910–1920* (Saltillo, Coahuila: Colegio Editorial del Estado, 1996). This work contains several hundred telegrams between Carranza and his military, civilian, and diplomatic principals on both sides of the international border. It is clear from these communications that Carranza was successful in establishing central government authority in this region.

CHAPTER 2

1 Alvaro Obregón, *Ocho mil kilómetros en campaña*, 3rd reprint (México, DF: Fondo de Cultura Económica, 1973). This work relates Obregón's military activities. It must, however, be read critically. See also Jean Meyer, Enrique Krauze, y Cayetano Reyes, *Historia de la Revolución Mexicana, 1924–1928* (México, DF: El Colegio de México, 1977).

2   For frontier conditions, see Héctor Aguilar Camín, *La frontera nomada: Sonora y la Revolución Méxicana* (México: DF: Siglo XXI Editores, 1977).

3   Linda B. Hall, *Alvaro Obregón: Power and Revolution in Mexico, 1911–1920*.

4   Jürgen Buchenau, *Plutarco Elías Calles and the Mexican Revolution* (Maryland: Rowman & Littlefield Publishers, 2007), p. xiii. This excellent and insightful work demonstrates how Calles's business background in Sonora, his teaching experience, social conditions in the state, and his family experiences shaped him for later life. See also Plutarco Elías Calles, *Pensamiento político y social: Antología: 1913–1936* (México, DF: Secretaría de Educación Pública, Fondo de Cultura Económica, 1988); Carlos Macías Richard, *Vida y temperamento: Plutarco Elías Calles, 1877–1920* (México, DF: Fideicomiso Archivos Plutarco Elías Calles y Fernando Torreblanca and Fondo de Cultura Económica, 1995); Macías Richard, "La fuerza del destino: Una biografía de Plutarco Elías Calles, 1877–1945." (Ph.D. diss., El Colegio de México, 1994); Lyle C. Brown, "The Calles-Cárdenas Connection," in *Twentieth Century Mexico*, ed. W. Dirk Raat and William H. Beezley (Lincoln: University of Nebraska Press, 1986), 146–158.

5   The documents in Dirección General de Investigaciónes Políticas y Sociales (DGIPS), Archivo General de la Nación (AGN) begin with exp. 1, tomo 1. In this volume the first communication is J. C. García to Jefe del Departamento Confidencial, México, DF, April 26, 1924. This is a cover letter for a note sent on to the president. In fact, the first three communications in the files contain little information of significance. Information from the Carrancista period is in VCT.

6   For intelligence gathering during the de la Huerta era, see Georgette José Valenzuela, "El secreto a voces que terminó en rebelión (septiembre–diciembre de 1923)," *Eslabones: Revista Semestral de Estudios Regionales* 2 (julio/diciembre, 1991): 159–162. See also Soledad García Morales, "Agentes confidenciales del tejedismo, 1920–1924," in ibid., 163–168.

7   Buchenau, *Plutarco Elías Calles*, 16.

8   Ibid., 28

9   Joaquín de la Peña to P. Elías Calles, Querétaro, September 28, 1924, exp. 70, Inv. 1393, Gav. 22, Fideicomiso Archivos Plutarco Elías Calles y Fernando Torreblanca, México, DF, hereafter cited as FAPEC.

10 "Informe," exp. 75, Gav. 70, Leg. 3/2/17, 134, FAPEC.

11 Martín F. Bárcenas to Subsecretario de Gobernación, December 6, 1924, exp. 25, Gav. 43, DGIPS.

12 For espionage and the Zuno-Calles conflict, see Jaime Tamayo y Fidelina G. Llerenas, "El espionaje político durante el conflicto Zuno-Calles," *Eslabones: Revista Semestral de Estudios Regionales* 2 (july/diciembre, 1991): 169–175.

13 Francisco M. Delgado to Secretario de Gobernación, México, DF, March 20, 1926, tomo 105, DGIPS.

14 *Excelsior*, México, DF, December 26 and 27, 1924; *El Universal*, México, DF, December 24, 1924.

15 Sánchez Aldama to Francisco Delgado, Guadalajara, Jalisco, April 3, 1926, tomo 105, DGIPS. See also *El Informador de Guadalajara*, Guadalajara, Jalisco, March 29, 1926.

16 Sánchez Aldama to Francisco Delgado, Guadalajara, Jalisco, April 7, 14, tomo 105, DGIPS.

17 Sánchez Aldama to Francisco Delgado, Guadalajara, Jalisco, May 8, 1926, tomo 105, ibid. See also *Excelsior*, México, DF, December 7, 1926.

18 Agent #17 to Francisco M. Delgado, México, DF, March 25, 1926, exp. 135, tomo 105, DGIPS; see also Teniente Coronel Salvador G. Galindo to Francisco M. Delgado, México, DF, April 23, 1926, ibid.

19 Agent #25 to Francisco M. Delgado, México, DF, January 25, 1926, exp. 75, Leg. 21/21, Inv. 5362, FAPEC.

20 Francisco M. Delgado to Agente #32, México, DF, October 23, 1928, exp. 342-369, tomo 105, DGIPS; see also Agente #32 to Francisco M. Delgado, October 28, 1928, ibid.

21 Agents 17 and 24 to Francisco M. Delgado, México, DF, September 5, 1928, exp. 5, tomo 60, ibid.

22 Emilio B. Zurita to Francisco M. Delgado, Guadalajara, Jalisco, September 19, 1928, exp. 16, tomo 60, ibid.

23 Emilio Zurita to Francisco M. Delgado, México, DF, October 15, 1928, exp. 16, tomo 60, ibid.

24 Agente #2 to Jefe del Departamento Confidencial, México, DF, January 19, 1932, exp. 3, tomo 2, ibid.

25 During this period, the agency adopted the names "Inspectors" and "Agents," which would be the standard used in future years. However, I will continue to use the term *agents* to avoid confusion.

CHAPTER 3

1 Enrique Garza García to Secretario de Gobernación, December 12, 1934, México, DF, exp. 17, tomo 43, DGIPS.

2 Lic. Salvador Estrada to Secretario de Gobernación, September 19, 1931, México, DF, exp. 17, tomo 43, DGIPS.

3 Corl. A. Torres Estrada to Sec. de Gobernación, April 29, 1932, México, DF, exp. 17, tomo 43, ibid.

4 Prof. Pastor C. Navarrete to Gral. P. E. Calles, México, DF, May 10, 1930, Pastor C. Navarrete, Inv. 3952, exp. 27, gav. 55, FAPEC. Letters relating to this are also in Quintana Valente, Inv. 4656, exp. 11, gav. 63, ibid.

5 Lic. Salvador Estrada Martínez to Sec. de Gobernación, México, DF, September 19, 1931, exp. 17, tomo 43, DGIPS.

6   Agente #11 to Jefe del Departamento, México, DF, January 7, 1932, exp. 3, tomo 2, ibid.

7   For examples of the reporting, see "Extractos de los Informes Rendidos con Esta Fecha por los Agentes de Este Departamento," July 15, 1931, México, DF, exp. 1, tomo 3, ibid.

8   Francisco M. Delgado to Calles, December 4, 1933, México, DF., Inv. 1427, exp. 104, gav. 22, FAPEC.

9   Enrique Durand F. to Abelardo L. Rodríguez, January 10, 1934, Tehuantepec, Oaxaca, exp. 6, tomo 108, DGIPS.

10 General Joaquín de la Peña to Secretario de Gobernación, May 11, 1934, México, DF, "Historia Institucional," exp. 1, tomo 44, ibid. See also, de la Peña, "Reglamento para el Funcionamiento Interior del Departamento Confidencial de la Secretaría de Gobernación," ibid.

11 Agent Hernández Bermúdez to Joaquín de la Peña, March 1, 1934, exp. 1, tomo 67, DGIPS.

12 Francisco García Vera to Joaquín de la Peña, México, DF, November 19, 1934, exp. 21, tomo 67, DGIPS.

13 Cárdenas has been the subject of numerous studies. General works include: Douglas Richmond, *The Mexican Nation: Historical Continuity and Modern Change* (Upper Saddle River, NJ: Prentice Hall, 2002); Michael J. Gonzales, *The Mexican Revolution, 1910–1940* (Albuquerque: University of New Mexico Press, 2002); Colin M. MacLachlan and William H. Beezley, *El Gran Pueblo: A History of Greater Mexico* (Upper Saddle River, NJ: Prentice Hall, 2004). More specifically, see Lyle C. Brown, "The Calles-Cárdenas Connection," in *Twentieth-Century Mexico*, ed. W. Dirk Raat and William H. Beezley, 146–158 (Lincoln: University of Nebraska Press, 1986). Adrian Bantjes, *As if Jesus Walked on Earth: Cardenismo, Sonora, and the Mexican Revolution* (Wilmington, DE: Scholarly Resources, 1998); George Wolfskill and Douglas W. Richmond, *Essays on the Mexican Revolution: Revisionist Views of the Leaders* (Austin: University of Texas Press, 1979); Lázaro Cárdenas, *Obras I-Apuntes 1913/1940* (México: DF: Universidad Nacional Autónoma de México, 1972.); Lázaro Cárdenas, Manuel Avila Camacho, Miguel Alemán Valdés, and Adolfo Ruiz Cortines, *Los Presidentes de México: Discursos políticos, 1910–1988*, tomo III (México, DF: El Colegio de México, 1988); Luis González, *Historia de la Revolución Mexicana, período, 1934–1940* (México, DF: Colegio de México, 1981).

14 Ignacio H. Santana to Estéban García de Alba, México, DF, March 13, 1936, exp. 1, tomo 72, DGIPS.

15 Ignacio H. Santana to Jefe de la Oficina, Durango, Durango, May 28, 1936, exp. 2, tomo 72, ibid.

16 See Alexander M. Saragoza, *The Monterrey Elite and the Mexican State, 1880–1940* (Austin: University of Texas Press, 1988).

17 Alfredo León to Jefe de DGIPS, México, DF, October 14, 1936, exp. 4, tomo 74,

DGIPS.

18 Herminio Lugo to Jefe de DGIPS, México, DF, October 27, 1936, exp. 7, tomo 74, ibid.

19 Capt. Salvador Amezcua F. to General Lázaro Cárdenas, México, DF, September 20, 1937, exp. 6, tomo 108, ibid.

20 Ignacio H. Santana to Jefe de DGIPS, Durango, Durango, May 28, 1936, exp. 1, tomo 72, ibid.

21 L. Lozano García to Jefe de DGIPS, Acámbaro, Guanajuato., March 17, 1936, exp. 2, tomo 72, ibid.

22 Lozano García to Jefe de DGIPS, Tampico, Tamaulipas, May 31, 1936, exp. 1, tomo 72, ibid.

23 Jesús García Ramírez to Jefe de DGIPS, Tepic, Nayarit, June 23, 1936, exp. 3, tomo 72, ibid.

24 Cipriano Arriola to Agent PS-12, México, DF, September 21, 1939, tomo 79, exp. 2 tomo 68, ibid.

25 Eliseo Castro Reina to Jefe de DGIPS, Puebla, Puebla, May 13, 1936, exp. 2 , tomo 68, ibid.

26 Eliseo Castro Reina to Jefe de DGIPS, México, DF, March 7, 1935, exp. 2, tomo 68, ibid.

27 Eliseo Castro Reina to Jefe de DGIPS, Canatlán, Durango, May 25, 1936, exp. 2, tomo 68, 1936, ibid.

28 See Friedrich E. Schuler, *Mexico Between Hitler and Roosevelt: Mexican Foreign Relations in the Age of Lázaro Cárdenas, 1934-1940* (Albuquerque: University of New Mexico Press, 1998). I have relied on Schuler's interpretation for I believe it to be accurate in respect to Cárdenas and leftist policies.

29 For additional information concerning the activities of Cedillo, see Archivo Local de Generales: General Saturnino Cedillo, XI/III/1-244, 5 tomos, 844 documentos, Archivo Histórico de la Defensa Nacional, México, DF, hereafter cited as AHDN. See also Dudley Ankerson, *Agrarian Warlord: Saturnino Cedillo and the Mexican Revolution in San Luis Potosí* (DeKalb, IL: Northern Illinois Press, 1984).

30 For an excellent work on San Luis Potosí, and Cedillo's role there, see Romana Falcón, *Revolución y caciquismo: San Luis Potosí, 1910-1938*. El Colegio de México, 1984. See especially 231–270.

31 Agente #2 to Jefe del Departamento, México, DF, June 3, 1933, exp. 24, tomo 30, DGIPS.

32 General Manuel Avila Camacho to Cedillo, México, DF, April 4, 1938, exp. XI/III/1-244, AHDN; Cedillo to General Lázaro Cárdenas, San Luis Potosí, San Luis Potosí, May 8, 1938, ibid.

33 Manuel Avila Camacho to Cedillo, México, DF, May 18, 1938, exp. XIII/I-244, AHDN. The Cedillo file in AHDN is 5 volumes, 844 documents, detailing Cedillo's career and his revolt.

34 Sargento First Class Alejandro Peña to General Lázaro Cárdenas, Tampico, Tamaulipas, October 15, 1937, Exp. XI/III/I-244, Clasificación 1-36, AHDN.
35 *Diario Oficial: Organo del Gobierno Constitucional de los Estados Unidos Mexicanos*, Sección Segunda, México, DF, August 25, 1938, núm. 48, 7-8, tomo CIX, AGN.
36 Francisco Urrutia to Jefe de DGIPS, Hermosillo, Sonora, August 18, 1938, exp. 5, tomo 5, fs 1-9, DGIPS.
37 Francisco Martínez Flores to Jefe de DGIPS, Nuevo Laredo, Tamaulipas, May 27, 28, and 31, 1938, exp. 1, tomo 77, ibid.
38 Francisco Urrutia to Jefe de DGIPS, Nuevo Laredo, Tamaulipas, April 18, 19, 1938, exp. 1, tomo 76, ibid. (A very few of the reports were signed as a second signature by agent #5. I cannot identify this agent).
39 Francisco Urrutia to Jefe de DGIPS, Acambaro, Guanajuato, May 13, 1938, exp. 1, tomo 76, ibid.
40 Francisco Urrutia to Jefe de DGIPS, Acámbaro, Guanajuato, May 13, 14, 1938, exp. 1, tomo 76, DGIPS.
41 Francisco Urrutia to Jefe de DGIPS, México, DF, January 5, 1938, exp.1, tomo 76, ibid.
42 Francisco Urrutia to Jefe de DGIPS, Mexico City, September 4, 18, 1938, exp. 1, tomo 139, ibid. See also, Francisco Urrutia to Jefe de DGIPS, Hermosillo, Sonora, August 19, 1938, exp. 5, tomo 5, ibid.
43 Antonio Méndez Coronado to Jefe de DGIPS, Parral, Chihuahua, August 26, 1938, exp. 7, tomo 5, ibid.
44 Ignacio García Tellez to Srta. Amada Bazán Nava, México, DF, September 16, 1938, exp. 31, tomo 82, ibid.
45 Amada Bazán Nava to Jefe de DGIPS, San Luis Potosí, SLP, October 11, 18, 1938, exp. 31, tomo 82, ibid.
46 Amada Bazán Nava to Jefe de DGIPS, San Luis Potosí, SLP, November 4, 5, and 24, 1938, exp. 31, tomo 82, ibid.
47 Agente #4 to Jefe del DGIPS, México, DF, January 23, 1939, exp. 5, tomo 83, ibid. This document is a multipage report of what agents learned before Cedillo died. The report contains the details of how he died.
48 See telegrams: Amada Bazán to Jefe de DGIPS, November 24, 25, 1938, and Jefe de DGIPS to Amada Bazán Nava, México, DF, December 2, 1938, all in exp. 31, tomo 82, ibid.
49 Francisco Martínez Flores to Jefe de DGIPS, Minatitlán, Veracruz, January 22, 1938, exp. 1, tomo 77, ibid.
50 Francisco Martínez Flores to Jefe de DGIPS, Villahermosa, Tabasco, January 27, 1938, exp. 1, tomo 77, ibid.
51 Ibid.
52 Aaron W. Navarro, "From Praetor to Pillar: The Military in Mexican Politics, 1938–1940," paper presented at the Southwest Conference on Latin American Studies, Veracruz, Mexico, March 9–12, 2005. Navarro investigates how Mexico

moved from an army general dominated presidency to a civilian leader.

53 Francisco Urrutia to Jefe de DGIPS, Saltillo, Coahuila, May 1, 1939, exp. 4, F.1-15, tomo 76, DGIPS.

54 Francisco Urrutia to Jefe de DGIPS, Torreón, Coahuila, 4, 1939, exp. 1-15, tomo 76, ibid.

55 V. C. Carranza to Jefe de DGIPS, México, DF, September 18, 1938, exp. 1, tomo 139, ibid.

56 Francisco Martínez Flores to Jefe de DGIPS, Monterrey, Nuevo León, June 15, 19, 20, and 30; July 6, exp. 3, tomo 77, ibid.

57 Francisco J. Martínez Flores to Jefe de DGIPS, México, DF, December 10, 1940, exp. 2.1/268.8/1, tomo 128, "Vigilancia, DGIPS."

58 For information about Almazán, see General Juan Andreu Almazán, Archivo Local de Generales, XI/III/1-114, 6 tomos, AHDN, México, DF See also Josefina Moguel Flores, *Juan Andreu Almazán* (México, DF: Editorial Planeta, 2002).

59 Juan Andreu Almazán to Secretario de la Defensa Nacional, Monterrey, Nuevo León, Exp. XI/III/II4, AHDN; see also Arsenio Jiménez to General Jesús Agustín Castro, Villahermosa, Tabasco, March 30, 1939, ibid. The General Juan Andreu Almazán file in the AHDN contains six volumes and 1,510 documents.

60 Francisco Martínez Flores to Jefe de DGIPS, Monterrey, Nuevo León, May 21, 25, 1940, exp. 3, tomo 77, DGIPS.

61 Schuler, *Mexico Between Hitler and Roosevelt*, 153–154. Schuler comments about Amaro and his earlier efforts to professionalize the Mexican army.

62 Francisco Urrutia to Jefe de DGIPS, México, DF, November 1, 1939, exp. 4, f. 138-188, tomo 76, DGIPS.

63 Cipriano Arriola to Jefe de DGIPS, México, DF, September 21, 1939, ibid.

64 José M. Clavé to Jefe de DGIPS, México, DF, August 20, 1939, exp. 20, tomo 141, ibid.

65 Fondo Presidentes: Lázaro Cárdenas, Informe confidencial al Presidente de la República, México, DF, August 12, 1940, 544. I/34-33, AGN.

66 José M. Clavé to Jefe de DGIPS, Saltillo, Coahuila, May 3, 1939, exp. 8, tomo 138, DGIPS.

67 Agent Jesús González Valencia to Jefe de DGIPS, Torreón, Coahuila, June 30, 1941, exp.10, tomo 138, ibid.

68 Erwin Friedeberg to Jefe de DGIPS, Acapulco, Guerrero, February 9, 1940, exp. 10, tomo 83, ibid.

69 Gustavo Abel Hernández Enríquez, and Armando Rojas Trujillo, *Manuel Avila Camacho: Biografía de un revolucionario con historia*, 2 tomos (Puebla: Ediciones del Gobierno del Estado de Puebla, 1986).This work contains considerable information about Avila Camacho's candidacy for the presidency and about his wartime leadership. It is not objective.

70 Stephen R. Niblo, *Mexico in the 1940s: Modernity, Politics, and Corruption* (Wilmington, DE: Scholarly Resources, 1999). This is an excellent treatment of

the period that offers basic information as well as an interpretation of the events. I have relied upon this work for much of my understanding of the 1940s. For a sound overview of the period 1910 to 1940, see also Michael J. Gonzalez, *The Mexican Revolution, 1910–1940*. (Albuquerque: University of New Mexico Press, 2002).

CHAPTER 4

1   Gustavo Abel Hernández Enríquez and Armando Rojas Trujillo, *Manuel Avila Camacho: Biografía de un revolucionario con historia*, 2 tomos (Puebla, México: Ediciones del Gobierno del Estado de Puebla, 1986).
2   For more on espionage and the World War II period, see María Emilia Paz, *Strategy, Security, and Spies: Mexico and the U.S. as Allies in World War II* (University Park, PA: Pennsylvania State University Press, 1997); see also, Joseph A. Stout Jr., "Estados Unidos y México durante la Segunda Guerra Mundial: El trato a japoneses, alemanes, e italianos," *Istor, año IV* 13 (verano del 2003): 61–79.
3   Héctor Aguilar Camín, *Saldos de la revolución: Cultura y política de México, 1910–1980* (México, DF: Editorial Nueva Imagen, 1982); see also Aguilar Camín and Lorenzo Meyer, *In the Shadow of the Mexican Revolution: Contemporary Mexican History, 1910–1989* (Austin: University of Texas Press, 1993). These works are similar, but each offers important insights into this period.
4   Hernández Enríques and Rojas Trujillo, *Manuel Avila Camacho*, tomo II, 45–47. Aaron W. Navarro, *Political Intelligence and the Creation of Modern Mexico, 1938-1954* (The Pennsylvania State University Press, 2010). Navarro ably explains the political intelligence work of the Departamento Confidencial during the years of Avila Camacho's presidency. The agency continued to be the tool of the president in respect to monitoring political opposition of all types.
5   *El Nacional*, México, DF, December 11, 12, and 21, 1941.
6   *Excelsior*, México, DF, May 15 and 23, 1942. See also, Stephen R. Niblo, *War, Diplomacy, and Development: The United States and Mexico, 1938–1954* (Wilmington, Delaware: Scholarly Resources Books, 1995),77–78; Blanca Torres Ramírez, *México en la Segunda Guerra Mundial, Período 1940–1952* (México, DF: El Colegio de México, 1979); Luis Medina, *Historia de la Revolución Méxicana, 1940–1952: Civilismo y modernización del autoritarismo*, tomo 20 (México: DF: El Colegio de México, segunda de reimpressión, 1995); Blanca Torres Ramírez, *Historia de la Revolución Mexicana, 1940–1952: Hacia la utopia industrial*, tomo 21, primera ed. (México, DF: El Colegio de México, 1984); Luis Medina, *Historia de la Revolución Mexicana, 1940–1952: Del cardenismo al avilacamachismo*, tomo 18 (México, DF: El Colegio de México, segunda reimpressión, 1996).
7   See newspaper clippings from Argentina and other information in Archivo

Histórico de La Secretaría de Relaciones Exteriores, 111–911-1, parte 1, México, DF.

8 *Excelsior*, México, DF, May 17, 1942. Research has shown that Germany and Japan had secret agendas using emigrants and sending agents to influence Mexican politics, or to establish potential bases of operation in preparation for possible war against either the United States or Britain. Two excellent works detail this posturing. See Friedrich E. Schuler, *Secret Wars and Secret Policies in the Americas, 1842-1929* (Albuquerque: University of New Mexico Press, 2010). See also Friedrich Katz, *The Secret War in Mexico* (Chicago: University of Chicago Press, 1981).

9 Studies of Mexican petroleum and the problems between the United States and Mexico between 1938 and the end of 1941 are numerous. See, for example, Jonathan C. Brown and Alan Knight, eds., *The Mexican Petroleum Industry in the Twentieth Century* (Austin: University of Texas Press, 1992); Lorenzo Meyer, *Mexico and the United States in the Oil Controversy, 1917–1942*, translated by Muriel Vasconcelos (Austin: University of Texas Press, 1977).

10 Meyer, *Mexico and the United States in the Oil Controversy*, 209–210.

11 Approximately six hundred pages of Departamento Confidencial records dealing with the Spanish Falange are located in tomo 142, exp. 1 and 2, 1939, DGIPS.

12 Agents PS-10 and PS-24 to Jefe del Departamento, México, DF, May 23, 1940, tomo 83, exp. 10, DGIPS. This is an unusually complete report, entitled "Nazismo en México," that is thirty pages long. Most agent reports are only a few pages and not as detailed as this one. Agents also analyzed the relationship of the Nazis in Mexico to Saturnino Cedillo, the Dorados, the Falange, and the Sinarquistas.

13 Schuler, *Mexico between Hitler and Roosevelt: Mexican Foreign Relations in the Age of Lázaro Cárdenas, 1934–1940*, 104.

14 Pierre de L. Boal, Chargé d'Affaires Ad Interim of the United States, to Secretary of State, May 31, 1940, México, DF, Washington, DC, Confidential United States State Department Central Files: Mexico Internal Affairs, 1940–1944, RG-59, Reel 18, part 1, 812.00N/LH, hereafter cited as NARS. Boal was not an unbiased observer, and what he says must be taken as potential fact, but sometimes pure speculation. Generally, however, he was correct in respect to German activities in Mexico, especially before war began in Europe in 1939.

15 See W. Dirk Raat, *Mexico and the United States: Ambivalent Vistas* (Athens, GA: University of Georgia Press, 1992). This work contains a great deal of information about the activities of agents of various countries.

16 See, for example, Herbert Hoover to Adolf A. Berle, Asst. Sec. of State, Washington, DC, April 8, 1940, RG-59, Reel 18, 812.00N/112LH, US National Archives and Records Service, Washington, DC.

17 Alfonso Taracena, *História Extraoficial de la Revolución Mexicana, desde las postrimerías del Porfirismo hasta sucesos de nuestros días* (México, DF: Editorial

Jus, 1972).

18 Pierre de L. Boal, to Secretary of State, México, DF, 812.00N/133, #10656, NARS.

19 Leslie B. Rout and John F. Bratzel, *The Shadow War: German Espionage and United States Counter Espionage in Latin America during World War II* (Frederick, MD: University Publications of America, 1986), 3–19.

20 See José Lelo de Larrea Domínguez: Su Expediente, 14-24-36, Archivo Histórico Genaro Estrada de la Secretaría de Relaciones Exteriores, [Mexico City] hereafter cited as AHSRE.

21 Ernesto Hidalgo of SRE, Secretario de Gobernación, México, DF, August 6, 1941, 111-610-23, AHSRE. See also "Alemanes que Pretenden Internarse en México," IV-705-12, AHSRE.

22 For an interesting overview of German espionage during World War I, and comments about German espionage during the 1930s up to 1941, see a 247-page text originally published in the *New York Times*, by Curt Riess. This manuscript is in Manuel Avila Camacho, ramo Presidencial, 545.3/44, AGN.

23 *El Nacional*, México, DF, December 12, 1941.

24 Ezequiel Padilla, Secretario de Relaciones Exteriores, to Miguel Alemán, Secretario de Gobernación, December 15, 1941, 111-610-23, núm. 81917, AHSRE. See also *El Nacional*, México, DF, December 9, 1941.

25 *El Nacional*, México, DF, December 11, 1941.

26 For additional information on this action, see 111-914-7, AHSRE.

27 Moisés González Navarro, *La colonización en México, 1877–1910* (México, DF: Talleres de Impresión de Estampillas y Valores, 1960). Much of the information for this section is based on this excellent work. In subsequent sections I have used only secondary sources in order to craft some framework for the study.

28 For an example of Italian settlement, see José Benigno Zilli Manica, *La Villa Luisa de los Italianos: Un proyecto liberal* (Biblioteca Universidad Veracruzana: Xalapa, Ver., 1997).

29 María Elena Ota Mishima, ed., *Destino México: Un estudio de las migraciones asiáticas a México* (México, DF: El Colegio de México, 1997). See also María Elena Ota Mishima, *Siete migraciones japonesas en México, 1890–1978* (México, DF: El Colegio de México, 1982). As is the instance with other groups immigrating to Mexico, I have used the careful work of Ota Mishima on the Japanese in Mexico. It is a significant contribution to Mexican immigration history. See also Chizuko Watanabe, "The Japanese Immigrant Community in Mexico: Its Past and Present" (master's thesis, California State University, Los Angeles, 1983).

30 Katz, *The Secret War in Mexico: Europe, the United States, and the Mexican Revolution*.

31 Alfredo Arriola Molina to Manuel Avila Camacho, Veracruz, Veracruz, December 9, 1941, 550/9, núm. 64275, Ramo Manuel Avila Camacho, Archivo General de la Nación, hereafter cited as RMAC.

32 Jesús Vargas Ruiz to Manuel Avila Camacho, Sayula, Jalisco, 550/9, núm. 64303, ibid.

33 Luciano P. Lara to Manuel Avila Camacho, Agua Dulce, Veracruz, December 24, 1941, 550/9, Núm. 66082, ibid.

34 US Ambassador to SRE, México, DF, April 28, 1943, Núm. 1216, 111-908-2, parte 1, AHSRE.

35 Jesús E. Dueñas, Secretario General de la Sección 65 del Sindicato Nacional de Mineros, Cananea, Sonora, to Avila Camacho, August 13, 1942, ibid.

36 Teresa López, Silvina López to Avila Camacho, El Salitre, Sinaloa, July 31, 1941, 545.3/44, RMAC.

37 Jorge Gálvez, Presidente del Comité de la Defensa Civil del Pueblo Yaqui, Sonora, to Lic. Jesús González Gallo, Secretario Particular de Avila Camacho, March 2, 1943, ibid.

38 J. Jesús Méndez Múgica to Avila Camacho, San Pedro, Coahuila, July 21 and 22, 1942, 550/9-8, ibid.

39 José Ibarra Silva to Manuel Avila Camacho, Minatitlán, Veracruz, December 14, 1941, 550/9, Núm. 65629, ibid.

40 Torres Ramírez, *México en la Segunda Guerra Mundial*.

41 *Diario Oficial*, México, DF, December 17, 1941, tomo cxxix, núm. 39, 1–16.

42 *El Nacional*, México, DF, December 21 and 22, 1941.

43 Betty Kirk, *Covering the Mexican Front: The Battle of Europe versus America* (Norman: University of Oklahoma Press, 1942).

44 Lic. Rafael Murillo Vidal to Manuel Avila Camacho, San Luis Potosí, November 25, 1941, 550/9, núm. 11437, RMAC.

45 Jorge Cerdán, Governor of Jalapa, Veracruz, to Manuel Avila Camacho, Jalapa, December 10, 1941, 550/9, núm. 69277, ibid.

46 Pedro Muñéz Armenta, 3er Batallón de Infantería Naval, Icacos, Acapulco, Guanajuato., January 7, 1942, 550/9, núm. 1266, ibid.

47 Dr. Héctor Jori to Manuel Avila Camacho, Colima, Colima, March 1, 1942, 550/9, núm. 7951, ibid; see also Martiniano Pérez, Presidente del Comité Municipal del PRM Siltepec, DTO. de Mariscal, Chiapas, January 25, 1942, núm. 5642, ibid.

48 Nicasio Carrera, Pdte, del Comité Ejecutivo Agrario, "kilómetro 19," Municipio de Tampico Alto, Veracruz, January 14, 1942, 550-/9, núm. 2268, RMAC.

49 Miguel Z. Martínez, Inspector Gral. de Policía, to Gobernación, México, DF, June 3, 1942, 550/9, no núm., AHSRE.

50 Eduardo Ampudia V. to Insp. Rafael Román Alemán, México, DF, January 3, 1945, exp 2-1/362 43/140, tomo 390, DGIPS.

51 Federico Nolde to Secretario de Gobernación, México, DF, May 8, 1945, ibid.

52 Federico Nolde to Secretario de Relaciones Exteriores, Atzala Municipio de Tlacotepec de Díaz, Puebla, September 16, 1949, ibid.

53 Diario Oficial: Organo del Gobierno Constitucional de los Estados Unidos Mexi-

canos, January 24, 1942, tomo CXXX, núm. 12, 15-32, AHSRE.

54 *El Nacional*, México, DF, January 6, 1942. See also *Excelsior*, México, DF, May 27, 1942.

55 SRE to Secretario de Gobernación, México, DF, January 8, 1942, 111-2436-10, núm. 57465, AHSRE.

56 See correspondence in 111-2436-10, AHSRE.

57 *El Nacional*, México, DF, January 8, 1942.

58 Ibid, January 20, 1942.

59 See decrees of the Mexican government, December 7 and 11, 1941, in 111-914-7, AHSRE.

60 Antonio de P. Araujo to Alfonso García González, Jefe del Departamento, Coatzacoalcos, Veracruz, March 31, 1942, exp. 2-1/362 (c52)/886, tomo 358, DGIPS.

61 Antonio de P. Araujo to Lic. Lelo de Larrea, Jefe del Departamento, México, DF, July 23, 1942, exp. 2-1/362(c52)/886, tomo 367, ibid.

62 Antonio de P. Araujo to Lic. Lelo de Larrea, Jefe del Depaartamento, Matías Romero, Oaxaca, October 10, 1942, ibid.

63 Adolfo Ruiz Cortines to La Junta de Administración y Vigilancia de la Propiedad Extranjera, México, DF, March 10, 1943, exp. 2-1/362-4 (52)591, tomo 362, ibid. This letter is one of several such communications concerning the Shimizu affair. The information in this long file also includes a number of memoranda concerning the Shimizu case.

64 Memorandum of the Comité Japonés de Ayuda Mútua to José Dos Santos Silva Taveira, Portuguese Embassy, México, DF, March 8, 1945, 111-917-6, AHSRE.

65 Lic. Pablo Campos Ortíz, Director General de Asuntos Políticos y del Servicio Diplomático, to Ramón Beteta, Secretario de Hacienda y Crédito Público, México, DF, September 30, 1944. See also Ramón Beteta to SRE, México, DF, June 24, 1944, both in 111-917-6, AHSRE.

66 *El Nacional*, México, DF, January 21, 1942.

67 Antonio Busterna Gagliani to chief of the DGIPS, Tijuana, Baja California, October 17, 1942, no exp. #, tomo 351, DGIPS.

68 Agent of Departamento Confidencial to Chief of the department, Tijuana, Baja California, October 16, 1942, ibid.

69 Maximiliano Torres to Miguel Alemán, Tijuana, Baja California, September 25, 1942, ibid.

70 José Lelo de Larrea Domínguez to Whomever it May Concern, México, DF, November 3, 1942, ibid.

71 Coronel Rodolfo Sánchez Taboada to Secretario de Gobernación, Tijuana, Baja California, November 11, 1942, ibid.

72 Lic. Rogerio de la Selva, Secretario Particular del C. Secretario de Gobernación, México, DF, September 3, 24, 1943, tomo 353, ibid. For more on Busterna Gagliani's attempt to become a naturalized Mexican, see Lic. Oscar Treviño Ríos, Dirección Gral. de Asuntos Jurídicos Oficina de Nac. Y Nat., México, DF, May

13, 1947, exp. 2-1/362.4(45)/365, tomo 2940, ibid.

73 General Fransico L. Urquizo to Secretario de Gobernación, México, DF, January 29, 1943, exp. 2-1/362-4 (45)/68, tomo 348, DGIPS.

74 Werner Barke to President Avila Camacho, May 5, 1942, Mexico, DF, 550-9-4, RMAC.

75 Luis Díaz Infante, Gobernación, to SRE, México, DF, February 12, 1946; see also Guillermo Schuppenhausen to SRE, México, DF, November 13, 1945, both in 111-675-24, AHSRE.

76 Lamberto Ortega Peregrina, Jefe del Depto. Demográfico, México, DF, November 8, 1950, exp. 2-1/326.6(A)/2, tomo 386, DGIPS.

77 Insp. J. Jesús Pérez S. to Jefe del DGIPS, México, DF, December 9, 1942, exp. 2-1 AGD/D1, tomo 739, DGIPS. This report is part of a 92-page file on Dorner.

78 Memorandum in the papers of Manuel Avila Camacho, July 22, 1943, 550/9, RMAC.

79 Lelo de Larrea to all agents, Mexico, DF, August 6, 1942, exp. 2-1/36, tomo 388, DGIPS.

80 Agents Juan Sánchez de Tagle and José R. Gracián to Lelo de Larrea, México, DF, November 25, 1942, exp. 2-1/362.6, tomo 388, ibid.

81 Schuler, *Mexico between Hitler and Roosevelt*.

82 F. Blasco Fernández-Moreda to Lelo de Larrea, México, DF, February 17, 22, 1943, exp. 19, tomo 741, DGIPS.

83 Jaime Torres Bodet to DGIPS, México, DF, April 24, 1942, ibid.

84 F. Blasco y Fernández-Moreda to DGIPS, México, DF, February 17, 23, 1943, ibid.

85 Lelo de Larrea to Insp. Roberto Ramos Castañeda, México, DF, July 16, 1943, ibid.

86 Agent Adi Stachlovici to Lelo de Larrea, México, DF, September 18 and October 13, 1943, ibid.

87 Lelo de Larrea to Antonia Elsa Martínez, Jesús Ibarra Esparza, Roberto Ramos Casteñeda, Adi Stachlovici, México, DF, July 16, 1943, ibid.

88 Agent Adi Stachlovici to Lelo de Larrea, México, DF, July 21, 1943, ibid.

89 Agent Adi Stachlovici to Lelo de Larrea, México, DF, July 21, 1943, September 7, ibid.

90 Agent Adi Stachlovici to Lelo de Larrea, México, DF, May 1944, ibid.

CHAPTER 5

1 Perhaps the best work providing insight into the DFS, and explaining operations of the DGIPS after 1947, is Sergio Aguayo Quezada, *1968: Los archivos de la violencia* (México, D.F: Editorial Grijalbo, S. A. De C. V., 1998). See also

Sergio Aguayo Quezada y Bruce Michael Bagley, compiladores, *En busca de la seguridad perdida, aproximaciones a la seguridad nacional mexicana* (México, DF: Siglo Veintuno Editores, S. A. de C.V., 1990). Aguayo Quezada, who is a professor of political science at El Colegio de México, has completed considerable work along these same lines. All of his work merits close reading for any student of modern Mexico.

2   Navarro, *Political Intelligence.*

BIBLIOGRAPHY

PRIMARY SOURCES: MEXICO

Archivo de la Secretaría de la Defensa Nacional, México, DF: Archivo Cancelados
  Files of various army officers
Archivo General de la Nación, México, DF.
Archivo Histórico "Genaro Estrada," de la Secretaría de Relaciones Exteriores, México, DF.
Biblioteca Nacional de Antropología e Historia, México, DF.
Centro de Estudios de la Historia de México CARSO, México, DF.
  Archivo Venustiano Carranza
Diario Oficial: Organo del Gobierno Constitucional de los Estados Unidos Mexicanos.
Dirección General de Investigaciones Políticas y Sociales. There are approximately 3,000 boxes in this collection.
Fideicomiso Archivos Plutarco Elías Calles y Fernando Torreblanca
  Archivo Plutarco Elías Calles
  Fondo Alvaro Obregón
Fondo Presidentes: Lázaro Cárdenas, Manuel Avila Camacho, Obregón-Calles. Archivo General de la Nación.

PRIMARY SOURCES: UNITED STATES

United States Department of State: Confidential United States State Department Central Files: Mexico Internal Affairs, 1940–1944, RG-59, reel 18, part 1, 812.00, Washington, DC.

NEWSPAPERS

El Informador de Guadalajara
El Nacional, México, DF.
Excelsior, México, DF.
New York Times

SECONDARY SOURCES:

Anderson, Mark Cronlund. *Pancho Villa's Revolution by Headlines*. Norman: University of Oklahoma Press, 2000.
Andrew, Christopher. *For the President's Eyes Only: Secret Intelligence and the American Presidency from Washington to Bush*. New York: Harper Collins Publishers, 1995.
Arguayo Quezada, Sergio. *1968: Los archivos de violencia*. México, DF: Editorial Grijalbo, S. A. de C.V., 1998.

Arguayo Quezada, Sergio and Bruce Michael Bagley, compiladores. *En busca de la seguridad perdida: Aproximaciones a la seguridad nacional mexicana.* México, DF: Siglo Veintouno Editores, S. A. de C.V., 1990.

Albro, Ward S. *Always a Rebel: Ricardo Flores Magón and the Mexican Revolution.* Fort Worth: Texas Christian University Press, 1972.

Ankerson, Dudley. *Agrarian Warlord: Saturnino Cedillo and the Mexican Revolution in San Luis Potosí.* DeKalb, Illinois: Northern Illinois University Press, 1984.

Aragón, Agustín. *Porfirio Díaz: historico geografico.* 2 tomos. México, DF: Editora Intercontinental, nd.

Aguilar Camín, Héctor and Lorenzo Meyer. *In the Shadow of the Mexican Revolution: Contemporary Mexican History, 1910–1989.* Austin: University of Texas Press, 1993.

———. *La frontera nómada: Sonora y la Revolución Mexicana.* México, DF: Siglo XXI Editores, 1977.

———. *Saldos de la revolución: Cultura y Política de México, 1910-1980.* México, DF: Editorial Nuevo Imagen, 1982.

Bantjes, Adrian A. *As If Jesus Walked on Earth: Cardenismo, Sonora and the Mexican Revolution.* Wilmington, DE: Scholarly Resources, 1998.

Barron, John. *KGB: The Secret Work of Soviet Secret Agents.* New York: Bantam, 1974.

Beals, Carlton. *Porfirio Díaz: Dictator of Mexico.* Westport, CN: Greenwood Press, 1959.

Benjamin, Thomas and Mark Wasserman, eds. *Provinces of the Revolution: Essays on Regional Mexican History, 1910–1929.* Albuquerque: University of New Mexico Press, 1990.

Beezley, William H. *Insurgent Governor: Abraham González of Chihuahua.* Lincoln: University of Nebraska Press, 1973.

Browder, George C. *Hitler's Enforcers: The Gestapo and the SS Security Service in the Nazi Revolution,* New York: Oxford University Press, 1996.

Brown, Jonathan C. and Alan Knight, eds. *The Mexican Petroleum Industry in the Twentieth Century.* Austin: University of Texas Press, 1992.

Brown, Lyle C. "The Calles-Cárdenas Connection." In *Twentieth Century Mexico,* edited by W. Dirk Raat and William H. Beezley, 146-158. Lincoln: University of Nebraska Press, 1986.

Brunk, Samuel. *Emiliano Zapata! Revolution and Betrayal in Mexico.* Lincoln: University of Nebraska Press, 1995.

Buchenau, Jürgen. *Plutarco Elías Calles and the Mexican Revolution.* Lanham, Maryland: Rowman and Littlefield Publishers, 2007.

Calles, Plutarco Elías. *Pensamiento político y social: Antología: 1913–1936.* México, DF: Secretaría de Educación Pública: Fondo de Cultura Económica, 1988.

Cárdenas, Lázaro. *Obras: I-Apuntes, 1913–1940.* I. México: DF: Universidad Nacional Autónoma de México, 1972.

Castro, Pedro: *Alvaro Obregón: fuego cenizas de la Revolución Mexicana.* Mexico, DF: Consejo Nacional para la Cultura y las Artes, 2009.

Cervantes, Francisco José. "Ojos sobre el sur: Carranza y los Oaxaqueños." *Eslabones: Revista Semestral de Estudios Regionales* 2 (julio/diciembre): 134–140. México, DF, 1991.

DePalo, William A. Jr. *The Mexican National Army, 1822–1852.* College Station: Texas A&M University Press, 1997.

Falcón, Romana. *Revolución y caciquismo: San Luis Potosí, 1910–1938.* México, DF: El Colegio de México, 1984.

Fowler, Will. *Santa Anna of Mexico.* Lincoln: University of Nebraska Press, 2007.

García Morales, Soledad. "Agentes confidenciales del tejedismo, 1920–1924." *Eslabones, Revista Semestral de Estudios Regionales* 2 (julio/diciembre): 163–168. México, DF, 1991.

García Ugarte, Marta Eugenia. "El chisme en corto o el espionaje profesional en Querétaro." *Eslabones Revista Semstral de Estudios Regionales* 2 (julio/diciembre): 141–153. México, DF, 1991.

Garner, Paul. *Porfirio Díaz: Profiles in Power.* London: Longman, 2001.

Gilly, Adolfo. El cardenismo, una utopia Mexicana. México, D.F: Cal y Arena, 1994.

Gonzales, Luis. *Historia de la Revolución Mexicano, periódo 1934–1940.* México, D.F México, DF: El Colegio de México, 1981.

Gonzales, Michael J. *The Mexican Revolution, 1910–1940.* Albuquerque: University of New Mexico Press, 2002.

González Navarro, Moisés. *La colonización en México, 1877–1910.* México, DF: Talleres de Impresión de Estampillas y Valores, 1960.

Hall, Linda B. *Alvaro Obregón: Power and Revolution in Mexico, 1911–1920.* College Station: Texas A&M University Press, 1981.

Hamnett, Brian R. *Juárez.* London: Longman, 1994.

Hart, John Mason. *Revolutionary Mexico: The Coming and Process of the Mexican Revolution.* 2nd ed. Berkeley: University of California Press, 1977.

Hernández Enríquez, Gustavo Abel and Armando Rojas Trujillo. *Manuel Avila Camacho: Biografía de un revolucionario con historia.* 2 tomos. Puebla: Ediciones del Gobierno del Estado de Puebla, 1986.

Huntington, Samuel P. *Political Order in Changing Societies.* New Haven: Yale University Press, 1968.

Jeffreys-Jones, Rhodri. *The FBI: A History.* New Haven: Yale University Press, 2007

José Valenzuela, Georgette. "El secreto a voces que terminó en rebelión." *Eslabones: Revista Semestral de Estudios Regionales* 2 (julio/diciembre): 159–162. México, DF, 1991.

Katz, Friedrich. "El espionaje mexicano en Estados Unidos durante la Revolución." *Eslabones; Revista Semestral de Estudios Regionales* 2 (julio/diciembre): 8–15. México, DF, 1991.

———. *The Life and Times of Pancho Villa.* Stanford, CA: Stanford University Press, 1998.

————. *The Secret War in Mexico: Europe, the United States and the Mexican Revolution*. Chicago: The University of Chicago Press, 1981.

Kahn, David. *Hitler's Spies: German Military Intelligence in World War II*. New York: MacMillan Publishing, 1978.

Kessler, Ronald. *The Bureau: The Secret History of the FBI*. New York: St. Martin's Press, 2002.

Kirk, Betty. *Covering the Mexican Front: The Battle of Europe Verses America*. Norman: University of Oklahoma Press, 1942.

Knight, Alan. *The Mexican Revolution*. 2 vols. Cambridge: Cambridge University Press, 1986.

Macías Richard, Carlos. "La fuerza del destino: Una biografía de Plutarco Elías Calles, 1877-1945." Ph.D. thesis, El Colegio de México, 1994.

————. *Vida y temperamento: Plutarco Elías Calles, 1877–1920*. México, DF: Fideicomiso Archivos Plutarco Elías Calles y Fernando Torreblanca, and Fondo de Cultura Económica, 1995.

MacLachlan, Colin M. and William H. Beezley. *El Gran Pueblo: A History of Greater Mexico*. Upper Saddle River, NJ: Prentice Hall, 2004.

Medina, Luis. *Historia de la Revolución Mexicana, 1940–1952: Del Cardenismo al avilacamachismo*. México, DF.: El Colegio de México, 1996.

————. *Historia de la Revolución Mexicana, 1940–1952: Civilismo y modernazación del autoritarismo*. 20 tomos. México, DF: El Colegio de México, 1995.

Meyer, Lorenzo. *Mexico and the United States in the Oil Controversy, 1917–1942*. Austin: University of Texas Press, 1977.

Meyer, Jean, Enrique Krauze, y Cayetano Reyes. *Historia de la Revolución Mexicana, 1924–1928: Estado y Sociedad con Calles*. México, DF: El Colegio de México, 1977.

Meyer, Michael C. *Huerta: A Political Portrait*. Lincoln: University of Nebraska Press, 1972.

————. *Mexican Rebel: Pascual Orozco and the Mexican Revolution, 1910–1915*. Lincoln: University of Nebraska Press, 1967.

Moguel Flores, Josefina. *Venustiano Carranza: Antología*. México, DF: Instituto Nacional de Estudios Historicos de la Revolución Mexicana, 1986.

————. *Venustiano Carranza: Primer Jefe y Presidente*. Saltillo, Coahuila: Secretaría de Gobernación, 1995.

————. *Juan Andreu Almazán*. México, DF: Editorial Planeta, 2002.

————. *El Magonismo en Coahuila*. Monterrey, N.L.: Grafo Print Editores, S.A., 2006.

Navarro, Aaron W. "From Praeter to Pillar: The Military in Mexican Politics, 1935–1940." Paper presented at Southwest Conference on Latin American Studies. Veracruz, México, March 9–12, 2005.

Navarro, Aaron W. *Political Intelligence and the Creation of Modern Mexico, 1938-1954*. University Park: Pennsylvania State University Press, 2010.

Niblo, Stephen R. *War, Diplomacy, and Development: The United States and Mexico, 1938-1954*. Wilmington, DE: Scholarly Resources, 1995.

———. *Mexico in the 1940s: Modernity, Politics, and Corruption*. Wilmington, DE: Scholarly Resources, 1999.

Obregón, Alvaro. *Ocho mil kilómetros en campaña*. 3rd reprint. México, DF; Fondo de Cultura Económica, 1973.

Olivera, Ruth R. and Liliane Crété. *Life in Mexico Under Santa Anna, 1822-1855*. Norman: University of Oklahoma Press, 1991.

Ota Mishima, María Elena, ed. *Un estudio de las migraciones asiáticos a México*. México, DF: El Colegio de México, 1982.

———. *Siete migraciones japonesas en México, 1890-1978*. México, DF: El Colegio de México, 1982.

Paz, María Emilia. *Strategy, Security, and Spies: Mexico and the U.S. Allies in World War II*. University Park, PA: Pennsylvania State University Press, 1997.

Raat, W. Dirk. *Mexico and the United States: Ambivalent Vistas*. Athens, GA: University of Georgia Press, 1992.

———. *Revoltosos: Mexico's Rebels in the United States, 1903-1923*. College Station: Texas A&M University Press, 1981.

Richmond, Douglas. *The Mexican Nation: Historical Continuity and Modern Changes*. Upper Saddle River, NJ: Prentice Hall, 2002.

———. *La Frontera México-Estados Unidos durante la época revolucionaria, 1910-1920: Antología Documental*. Coahuila, México: Consejo Editorial del Estado, 1996.

———. *Venustiano Carranza's Nationalist Struggle, 1893-1920*. Lincoln: University of Nebraska Press, 1983.

Rout, Leslie B. and John F. Bratzel. *The Shadow War: German Espionage and United States Counterespionage in Latin America during World War II*. College Park, Maryland: University Publications of America, 1986.

Sandos, James A. *Rebellion in the Borderlands: Anarchism and the Plan of San Diego, 1904-1923*. Norman: University of Oklahoma Press, 1992.

Santoni, Pedro. *Mexicans at Arms: Puro Federalists and the Politics of War, 1845-1848*. Fort Worth: Texas Christian University Press, 1996.

Schuler, Friedrich E. *Mexico between Hitler and Roosevelt: Mexican Foreign Relations in the Age of Lázaro Cárdenas, 1934-1940*. Albuquerque: University of New Mexico Press, 1998.

———. *Secret Wars and Secret Policies in the Americas, 1842-1929*. Albuquerque: University of New Mexico Press, 2010.

Smith, Michael M. "Carrancista Propaganda and the Print Media in the United States: An Overview of Institutions." *The Americas* 52, no. 2 (October, 1995): 155-174.

———. "The Mexican Secret Service in the United States, 1910-1920." *The Americas* 59, no. 1 (July, 2002): 65-85.

———. "Gringo Propagandist: George F. Weeks and the Mexican Revolution." *Journalism History* 29 (Spring, 2003): 2-11.

———. "Andrés G. García: Venustiano Carranza's Eyes, Ears, and Voice on the Border." *Mexican Studies (Estudios Mexicanos)* 23, no. 2 (Summer, 2007): 355-414.

Stout, Joseph A. Jr. *Border Conflict: Villistas, Carrancistas, and the Punitive Expedition, 1916–1920*. Fort Worth: Texas Christian University Press, 1999.

———. "Estados Unidos y México durante la Segunda Guerra Mundial: El trato a japoneses, alemanes, e italianos." *Istor* IV, no. 13 (verano, 2003): 61–79.

———. "La expedición punitiva." *Provincias Internas* II, no. 7/8 (otoño e invierno, 2002–2003): 93–107.

Taracena, Alfonso. *Historia extra oficial de la Revolución Mexicana, desde las postremerías del porfirismo hasta los sucesos de nuestros días*. México, DF: Editorial Jus, 1972.

Tamayo, Jaime y Fidelina Llerenas. "El espionaje político durante el conflicto Zuno-Calles." *Eslabones: Revista Semestral de Estudios Regionales* 2 (julio/diciembre): 170–175 México, DF, 1991.

Torres, Blanca. *Historia de la Revolución Mexicana, 1940–1952: Hacia la utopia industrial*. Tomo 21, primera ed. México, DF: El Colegio de México, 1984.

———. *México en la Segunda Guerra Mundial período, 1940–1952*. México, DF: El Colegio de México, 1979.

Tinker-Salas, Miguel. *Shadow of the Eagles: Sonora and the Transformation of the Border during the Porfiriato*. Berkeley: University of California Press, 1977.

Vanderwood, Paul J. *Disorder and Progress: Bandits, Police, and Mexican Development*. Wilmington, DE: Scholarly Resources, 1992.

Vásquez, Josefina Z. "Benito Juárez y la consolidación del estado mexicano." In Abreu, Juana Inés, ed. *Juárez: Memoria e imagen*, 35. México, DF: Secretaría de Hacienda y Crédito Público, 1998.

Villalobos Calderón, Librorio. "Hacia una historia de la Secretaría de Gobernación." *Solo Historia* 2, no. 8 (abril–junio, 2000): 65–69.

Watanabe, Chizuko. "The Japanese Immigrant Community in Mexico: Its History and Present." Master's Thesis, California State University at Los Angeles, 1983.

Werne, Joseph R. *The Imaginary Line: A History of the United States and Mexican Boundary Survey*, 1848–1857. Fort Worth: Texas Christian University Press, 2007.

Wolfskill, George and Douglas Richmond. *Essays on the Mexican Revolution: Revisionist Views of the Leaders*. Austin: University of Texas Press, 1979.

Wasserman, Mark. *Persistent Oligarchs: Elites and Politics in Chihuahua, Mexico, 1910–1940*. Durham, NC: Duke University Press, 1993.

Womack, John Jr. *Zapata and the Mexican Revolution*. New York: Alfred A. Knopf, 1969.

Zilli Manica, José Benigno. *La Villa Luisa de los Italianos: Un proyecto liberal*. Xalapa, Veracruz: Biblioteca Universidad Veracruzana, 1997.

INDEX

Acuña, Jesús, 20
Adamik, George, 126
Agentes de Información, mentioned, 43, 75
Agricultural School of Chapingo, Saturnino Cedillo confronts President Lázaro Cárdenas, 83
Aguirre Colorado, General Ernesto, 95
Aldama, Sánchez, 46
Aguirre Berlanga, Manuel, 21, 22
Alemán Valdés, Miguel, as president, 140; as Secretario de Gobernación, 118, 138; orders Japanese inland from Baja California, 128, 133-134
Almazán, General Juan Andreu, 35; sides with Calles in 1929, 54; relations with Cárdenas, 74, 95-97, 100-103, 106
Amaro, General Joaquín, 35, 53, 96, 97, 143; photo, 55
Amezcua F., Capt. Salvador, 75
Amieva Noceda, Pedro, 139
Araujo, Antonio de P., 129-131
Army revolt of 1923, 35-36
Arriola, Cipriano, 79, 92-94, 102
Arriola, Jesús M., and the Mexican Bureau of Investigation, 22
Arriola Molina, Alfredo, 124
Ashida, Federico, 126
Avila Camacho, Manuel, 78, 84; Cárdenas supports for president, 96, 98, 100-104; assumes presidency, 105-107, 110-115, 119, 124, 134-135; outlaws Sinarquistas, 140, 143; photos, 106, 108
Avila Camacho, Maximino, 78-79, 111; and graft, 137; photos, 107, 108

Axis groups, Mexico takes action against, 128-129
Bárcenas, Martín F., 40-42
Barke, Werner, 134-135
Bartlett Bautista, Manuel, 95
Bazán Nava, Amada, 91-94
Beas Mendoza, Major Francisco, 64-65
Benjamin, Thomas, viii
Blanco, General Lucio, 47
Blumenthal Schwab, Federico, 136
Blumenthal Schwab, Matilda, 136
Bonillas, Ignacio, 1, 27, 68
Buchenau, Jürgen, 33, 37
Busterna Gagliani, Antonio, 132-133
Buve, Raymond Th. J., viii
Cabrera, Capitán Pablo, 130
Calles, Plutarco Elías, ix, 1-2, 12, 27, 28, 33-41, 43-44, 47-48, 142-143; anticlerical attitudes, 49; actions against Cristeros, 50, 52-54; and the Partido Nacional Revolucionario, 56-61; and government influence, 64, 66-69; and Cardenas, 70-71, 74-75; and Saturnino Cedillo, 81; photos, 26, 38, 45, 49, 50, 61, 106
Camisas Doradas, 82, 89-90, 111
Canaris, Admiral W. F., Chief of Abwehr, 7, 119
Cantisani Peluso, José, 134
Cárdenas, General Lázaro, ix, 35, 142; as Secretario de Gobernación, 41; sides with Calles in revolt of 1929, 54, 58-59, 66, 69-70; moves to end the influence of Calles, 71-72; exiles Calles, 72-73; travels through northern frontier, 96-98, 101; and nationalization of petroleum, 73, 74-77, 87,

109, 114; drug smuggling, 89; photos, 106, 107

Cárdenas, Raquel, 58

Carranza, Venustiano, 1, 17; and secret service, 19, 20, 21, 22, 26, 27, 34; Catholic Church and the Mexican government, 1, 12, 15, 33, 40, 68; and Saturnino Cedillo, 81, 105, 142; photos, 26, 29

Carrillo, José Enrique, 139

Casa de Detención, 134

Casa de España, México, 138

Castro Reina, Eliseo, 78-80, 87

Catholic Church, monitored, 12, 47, 49-50, 65

Cayetano, Juan, 127

Cedillo, Elena, 93

Cedillo, General Saturnino, 80-90, 92-94, 96, 116

Celorio Sordo, Eulogio, 139

Chávez Sierra, David, 62

Clavé, José M., 102-103

Columbus, New Mexico, villista attack, 22

Communists, 3, 9, 33, 61, 63-64, 68, 82, 97, 103, 110

Confederación Campesina Mexicana, 77

Confederación de la Clase Media, 82

Confederación de Sociedades Ferrocarrileras de la República Mexicana, 48

Confederación de Trabajadores de México, (CTM), 80, 83, 91, 98, 111

Confederación Patronal de la República Mexicana, 74

Confederación Regional Obreras Mexicanas (CROM), 31, 33, 38, 44, 80, 98, 111; monitoring of, 59-60; Zuno attacks, 46, 48-49

Consejo de Hispanidad, 140

Constitution of 1917, 27, 33, 35, 46, 52, 121

Constitutionalists, 19, photo, 24

Contreras, Luis González, 62

Corona Benavides, J. Guadalupe, 91

Creel, Enrique, and the Terrazas family, 17

Cristero Rebellion, 76; and Calles, 12, 49, 51-52, 54, 60; photo, 52

De la Huerta, General Victoriano Adolfo, 27, 28; revolts against Obregón, 35-36, 44, 46; loyalists along the Mexican-US border, 47, 81

De la Luz Mena, José, 62

De la Peña, General Joaquín, 39, 67

De Montaño, María Cepeda, 79

Delgado, Col. Francisco M., 43, 47, 54, 56, 66; and Cristero rebellion, 50-51; and organization of Departamento Confidencial, 57-58

Departamento Confidencial, Calles established, 33-34

Departamento de Investigaciones Políticas y Sociales, 85

Departamento de Publicidad y Propaganda, mentioned, 75

Díaz, General Félix, 17

Díaz, General Porfirio, viii, 1, 15, 16, 27, 37, 110, 142; and use of consular agents as a secret service, 16-17; abdication of presidency, 17; and immigration, 121-123

Diéguez, General Manuel M., 35

Dirección de Investigaciones y Seguridad Nacional (DISEN), created, 144

Dirección del Servicio Secreto, mentioned, 75

Dirección Federal de Seguridad (DFS) created, 144

Dirección General de Investigaciones Políticas y Sociales (DGIPS), 34, 142, 145

Dietrich, Arthur, 116-118

Dorner, Herman, 137

Drug dealers, Distrito Federal, 41; along the frontier, 89

Dueñas, Jesús E., 124

Durand, Dr. Enrique, 67

Echeverría Alvarez, Luis, 46, 145

El Casino Alemán, 117

El Colegio Alemán, 117

El Machete, Communist weekly, 68

Escobar, General José Gonzalo, 54, 88

Esquivel, Aureliano, 22

Estrada, General Enrique, 35, 44, 46

Estrada Martínez, Sálvador, 62, 65

Faja de Oro, German submarine destroyed, 113, leads to Mexico entering WWII, 113

Falcón, Romana, viii

Federal Bureau of Investigation (FBI) during 1908-1946, a clandestine organization in a democracy, 7-11, in Mexico, 117-118

Fernández Cejudo, Roberto, 102

Ferral, Lic. Jesús, 90

Figueroa, General Andrés, 52

Flores, Daniel, attempted assassination of Ortiz Rubio, 56

Flores, Rafael, 21, 40

Franco, General Francisco, 108, 111, 138-140

Frente Popular de Izquierda, 77

Frente Regional de Obreros y Campesinos, 78

Friedeberg, Erwin, 104

Furlong Secret Service Company, 17

Furlong, Thomas, 17

Galicia Ortega, David, 58

Gálvez, Jorge, 125

García, Andrés, and Mexican espionage in the U.S., 21-22; photo, 21

García, Lamberto, 21, 40

García Ramírez, Jesús, 77

García Tellez, Ignacio, 85

García, Trinidad, 58

Garner, Paul, viii

Garza García, Enrique, 61

Garza, Jesús E., 89

Gestapo, 6-7, 11-12; operatives in Mexico, 116-117, 119

Gobernación, Secretarío de, 2, 19, 21, 28, 33, 39, 41, 43-44, 56-57, 59-63, 65, 85, 96, 100, 143, 145; works with FBI, 118, 127-128; and wartime relocations, 131-135, 137, 138

Gómez, Arnulfo R., and revolt of 1929, 52-53

Gómez Velasco, General, 129-131

González, Alvarito, 135

González, Eleutario, 69

González, Manuel, 134-135

González, General Vicente, 35

González Contreras,Luis, 62

González de Betancourt, Dolores, 20

González Sánchez, Gildardo, and the Sinarchista movement, 98

González Valencia, Jesús, 103

Gonzalo Escobar, General José, 54, 88

Granados, Adolfo, 63

Gross, José, 90

Grupo de Agentes Especiales, suggested, 75

Guardias Rurales, 16

Guerra, Feliciano, (El Torero), drugs, 89

Guerrero, General Anacleto, 97

Gutiérrez, José Jesús, 58

Gutiérrez, Miguel, 21, 40

Guzmán, General Miguel H., and the death of Cedillo, 94

Hall, Linda B., 31

Hanson, Captain William, U. S. Department of Immigration, 47

Hidalgo y Castillo, Padre Miguel, 15

Hinojosa, Jesús, "La Mancha," drug king, 89

Hitler, Adolf, internal security under the National Socialist Party (NAZIS),

5-7, 101, 108-109, 115-116
Hoover, J. Edgar, 9; and Mexico, 118
Hopf, Ernst, 137
Huerta, General Victoriano, 1, 17-19, 22
Huerta, José, 139
Huntington, Samuel P., viii
Ibáñez Serrano, Agusto, 138-139
Immigration, Mexican Department of, 137
Immigration, US Department of, 47
Iturbide, Augustín, 15
Izquierdo, Eusebio, Federal District Police along the northern border, 47-48
Jaime Torres, Enrique, arms dealer, 88
Japan, attacks US beginning WWII, 10, 109
Jiménez, Lt. Col. Ignacio, murdered, 41
Jones, Gus T., US Department of Justice, 47, 118
Knights of Columbus, 64
Kohashi, Enrique F., 129-131
Krupp, House of, German industrial firm, 135
La Comunidad Popular Alemana, 116
La Liga Pro-cultura Alemana en México, 120
La Refinería de Minatitlán, 125
Lelo de Larrea Domínguez, José, 112, 119-120, 133, 138, 140
León, Alfredo, 74
León Toral, José de, kills Obregón, 54
Liga Femenil Leona Vicario, 124
Ligas Agrarias, 81
Loaiza, Col. Rodolfo T., 131
Lombardo Toledano, Vicente, 98
López, Jesús, 77
Lozano García, L., 76-77
Lugo, Herminio, 75
Madero, Francisco I., 1, 17, 68; photo, 18

Magón, Enrique, 16
Magón, Ricardo Flores, 16
Mancera Aldeco, Rafael, 62
Martínez, Antonia Elsa, woman agent, 140
Martínez Flores, Francisco, 87, 94-95, 99-101
Martínez, General Eugenio, 35
Martínez Vértiz, José, 69
Maycotte, General Fortunato, 35
Mayer, Col. Francisco, 58
Mayo Indians, 99
Méndez Corona, Antonio, 91
Meneses, Pablo, 57, 61-64, 65
Merced López, José, 58
Mexican Bureau of Investigation, 22
Miranda, Gabriel, 62-64
Moguel, Eduardo, 65
Moreno, Jesús, 21, 40
Morones, Luis N., 31, 33, 38, 44, 48-49, 59-60; photos, 49, 50, 61
Múgica, General Francisco J., 96-97
Natera, General Pánfilo, 20
Nava, Guilebaldo, 20
Navarrete, Pastor C., 57-58, 64
Navarro, Aaron, DGIPS and politics, 145
Navarro, General Paulino, 21, 40
Nicolaus, Georg, 138
Nogueda Radilla, Antonio, murdered, 104
Nolde, Federico, 126-127
Northe, Dr. Heinrich, 116
Obregón, Alvaro, ix, 1, 2, 17, 22, 27-28, 31, 33-36, 39-40, 44, 52-54, 60, 69, 70, 81, 142-143; photos, 21, 32, 50
Oficina Federal de Hacienda, 93
Oficina de Migración (Veracruz), 95
Oseki, Rafael, 126
Ortega, Lt. Col. Eufrasio, 42-43
Ortiz Rubio, Pascual, as president, 56, 60, 80; photo, 106

Partido Acción Nacional, (PAN), 97, 100

Partido Comunista Mexicano, (PCM), 110

Partido de la Revolución Mexicana (PRM), created from the PNR, 85, 107, 111

Partido del Obrero y Campesino Mexicano, 63

Partido Nacional Revolucionario (PNR), 59-60, 70, 74, 82, 85, 95; Calles creates, 1928, 54; monitored, 65

Partido Revolucionario Anti-Comunista (PRAC), 97

Partido Revolucionario de Unificación Nacional (PRUN), 96

Partido Revolucionario Institucional (PRI) created in 1946, 107

Partido Revolucionario Mexicano, 74, 76, 80, 85, 96, 100, 103, 107, 111

P. de Negri, Ramón, 22

Peña, Pablo, 89

Pérez Gallardo, General Raymundo, 92

Pérez Treviño, General Manuel, 97

Pershing, General John J., commands troops in Mexico, 22

Pfeiffer, Amalia, 138

Pfeiffer, Dr. Friedrich, 138

Plan de Agua Prieta, 27

Plan de Hermosillo, 54

Plan de Guadalupe, 17

Portes Gil, Emilio, as provisional president, 54, 60, 78; photo, 106

Potrero del Llano, Mexican oil tanker destroyed by German submarine, 112

Primo de Rivera, José, 138

Primo de Rivera, Miguel, 138

Querétaro, constituent congress of 1917, 26-27

Quintana, Valente, 64

Ramírez Martínez, Julia, 79

Rangel, Edmundo, murdered, 68

Regeneración, 16

Relaciones Exteriores, Secretaría de, ix, 19

Relocation or internment of Axis related individuals, vii, 10, 11, 113, 119, 124-140

Retelsdorf, Carlos, 126

Reyes, General Bernardo, 17

Riva Palacio, Carlos, cooperates with Calles, 56-57

Riva Palacio, Vicente, 121

Rodríguez, General Abelardo, as president, 56, 60, 64, 67, 69, 70; photo, 106

Rodríguez, Nicolás, 87, 90

Roosevelt, President Franklin D. (FDR), 8, 9, 10, 11, 115, 119; and the Good Neighbor Policy, 73, 109-110, 114; economic depression and New Deal, 107-108; and Mexican oil, 114

Rosas, Miguel, Monterrey policeman, and drug traffic, 99

Salamini, Heather F., viii

Sánchez, General Guadalupe, 35

Sánchez Taboada, Col. Rodolfo, 133

Santana, Ignacio H., 71, 76

Santos Moyano, General José, 90

Schuler, Friedrich, and German espionage in Mexico, 117

Schuppenhausen, Guillermo, 135

Schuppenhausen, Marta Alemán, 135

Secretaría de Comunicaciones, 102

Secretaría de Hacienda y Crédito Público, 125

Secretario de Comunicaciones y Obras Públicas, 111

Secretario de la Defensa Nacional, 84, 105

Secretario de las Relaciones Exteriores, (SRE), 120

Serrano, General Francisco R., 35; and the revolt of 1929, 52-53

Shiller, Mathias, 130

Shimizu, Dr. Toshio, 131-132
Shiyama, Mitori, 129
Sinarquista movement, 82, 98, 111, 112, 114, 140
Sindicato Nacional de Mineros, at Cananea, 124
Sociedad de Beneficencia Alemana, 135
Soledad Rodríguez, J., 20
Spanish Falange, 98, 111, 114, 138-140
Stalin, Josef, 101, 109; internal espionage in the Soviet Union, 3-5
Taquiuchi, Eduardo, 126
Tlaxcalantongo, Carranza murdered, 27
Tojo, Hideki, Japanese minister, 126
Torres Estrada, Col. Adalberto, 64
Tostado, Jesús A., 74, 78
Trauwitz, Margot, 116
Trujillo Gurría, Lic. Francisco, 95-96
Urquizo, General Francisco L., 134
Urrutia, Francisco, 86, 88-91, 97
Vadillo, Governor (Jalisco) Basilio, 44
Valenzuela, Gilberto, 39-40, 43
Valls, Sheriff John, Webb County, Texas, arrests Mexican police representative, 47-48
Velázquez, Ana María, 58
Villa, General Francisco (Pancho), 17, 19; at Battles of Celaya and León, 22, 28; killed at Parral, 36-37, photos, 23, 36, 37
Villista troops, photos, 23, 25, 36
von Collenberg, Barón Ruedt, German ambassador, 116
von Merck, Ernest, 87
Voss, Stuart, viii
Wallace, Henry A., VP of U. S., 115
Wasserman, Mark, viii-ix
Wilson, Carmen T., 126-127
Wilson Rey, Eduardo Miguel, 127
Wilson, President Woodrow, orders
troops to US-Mexican border, 22
Wirtz, Wilhelm, 116
Yanagihara, Arturo, 124
Yaqui Indians, 98-99
Yocupicio, General Román, 91, 99, talks with Germans, 116; photo of headquarters, 92
Zapata, General Emiliano, 17, 27, 35
Ziegler, Carlos, J., and sabotage, 125
Zimmermann Telegram, 20
Zubarán Capmany, Rafael, 19
Zuno, José Guadalupe, 44; opposes government, 46
Zurita, Emilio, Agent of the Departamento Confidencial, and the Cristeros, 51-52

ABOUT THE AUTHOR

Until his retirement in 2005, Joseph A. Stout Jr. was Regents Professor of History and held the Norris Professorship at Oklahoma State University. He has written or edited fourteen books and more than thirty articles on the American Southwest and Mexico. He has two previous books published by TCU Press: *Border Conflict: Villistas, Carrancistas, and the Punitive Expedition, 1915-1920*; and *Schemers and Dreamers: Filibustering in Mexico, 1848-1921*.

.